SECOND EDITION

CASINO CAMPING

GUIDE TO RV-FRIENDLY CASINOS

by Jane Kenny

Library of Congress Control Number: 2005911393
ISBN: 1-885464-14-2

CASINO CAMPING

For Jack: my pilot and my best friend

Contents

Introduction

Today, more than ever, the good news for RV gaming aficionados is: you don't have to trek all the way to Las Vegas or Atlantic City for your gaming fun. Casinos are all over the country and this book locates them for you. Gaming is growing rapidly in the U.S. and this casino guide reflects many changes in the 29 states listed.

A Guide To RV-Friendly Casinos

Casino Camping is primarily a guide for the many Americans who travel the country in recreational vehicles. Consequently, while the book includes *most* casinos in the country, some casinos are not listed because they are not accessible for recreational vehicles. Excluded from the text are casinos in remote locations that are too difficult for RVs to reach, and those in crowded metropolitan areas where RV parking is limited or restricted. Also excluded are casinos that do not allow RV parking.

It's important to note that this book has been compiled by RVers on the road. We will tell you which casinos welcome RVs and which ones don't want us!

Quite a few casino resorts have full service RV parks or are planning to add them to their facility. Those that don't have RV parks usually allow free overnight parking; some even have electric hookups for RVs in the parking lot. Shuttle service between the parking area and the casino is available at most large casinos.

Traveling players like to plan their trips to include a night or two of gaming while en route. Others will spend more time at a casino location if it has full service accommodations plus other attractions and recreation in the area.

Casino RV parks are growing in popularity as destinations for RV club rallies. A separate state-by-state location chart in the appendix section lists casinos that have RV parks, campgrounds or electric hookups. Most

RV parks at casino resorts are new and modern. Guests not only get to camp out next to the casino, but they can often enjoy other luxury amenities throughout the resort – pool/spa, sauna, fitness center, golf course, etc. Many casinos currently have an RV park in their plans for future expansion because market studies have indicated that gaming destination resorts will be as popular as fishing destinations for retirees in RVs.

How This Guide Is Organized

Following introductory articles, this book is organized alphabetically by state. A map at the beginning of each state section pinpoints casino locations. Individual listings are cross-referenced to the map by number. Each casino listing includes the following information where applicable:

- Name, address, phone numbers and web address,
- On site hotel or motel – number of rooms/suites,
- Amenities (pool, fitness room, business center, etc).
- RV park or campground and last year's rates,
- Restaurants on site,
- Entertainment,
- Golf course,
- Discounts generally offered at the casino resort,
- Casino description (slots, table games, poker room),
- Driving directions,
- Parking information for RVers.

A Word About Nevada and New Jersey

Nevada remains the casino capital of America with literally thousands of gaming sites throughout the state. And Nevada always has the welcome mat out for RVs. The Nevada section of this guide has details that will be of interest and value to everyone planning a trip to that state.

New Jersey's casinos are all located in Atlantic City, but there are no RV parks at any of the Atlantic City casinos. Furthermore, overnight parking is prohibited anywhere in the city (including casino parking lots) by local ordinance. The New Jersey section of this book features a description of the casino areas in Atlantic City for RVers who may want to go in for a "casino-hopping" day trip and for gaming enthusiasts planning an Atlantic City vacation.

Popular Gaming Destinations

Detailed descriptions of popular "casino hopping" destinations for RVers appear in the following state sections:

- Colorado – Black Hawk/Central City and Cripple Creek
- Connecticut – Foxwoods and Mohegan Sun
- Mississippi – Tunica County
- Nevada – Las Vegas, Laughlin and Reno
- South Dakota – Deadwood

We hope you will find the second edition of our book helpful and informative as you travel this beautiful land. Wishing you safe and happy travels.

Jane

Blacktop Boondocking Tips

Question: What is blacktop boondocking?

Answer: Free overnight parking for self-contained RVs, typically on the paved parking area of a business establishment, with the property owner's permission.

The key phrase in this definition is *"with the property owner's permission."* Consequently whenever RVers want to stay overnight in a parking lot they must obtain permission from the property owner. RVers who occasionally look for free overnight parking know that the places most inclined to permit blacktop boondocking in their parking lots are casinos, 24-hour super stores and truck stops.

If you wish to secure free overnight parking, it is important to obtain authorization from management or security personnel. The casinos listed in this book are all "RV-Friendly," that is they have an RV park and/or they permit free overnight parking in their lot. Blacktop boondocking at a casino is safe and secure. Casinos welcome adult campers because they know their facility is getting additional business. And the RVer gets a quiet, safe spot to rest and relax without being hassled. Since most casinos are open 24/7, security personnel are on duty all night.

But a parking lot is not a campground. When your RV is in for a free overnight stay, you are there because the property owners allow RV parking. Don't take advantage of their hospitality. During our travels we've observed blacktop boondockers who act like they own the parking lot. They put out the awning, set up table and chairs and break out the barbeque grill. Please remember, blacktop boondockers don't pay for their parking space. Therefore, the circumstances are different from a campground. When you rent a spot at a campground, you've paid for your site and you're entitled to make yourself at home – you "own" that campsite for the night. But when boondocking in a parking lot, be considerate of the property owner. Park in the area designated for RVs. If there is no specifically designated RV area, we suggest parking on the perimeter of the lot – don't take up spaces reserved for customers with cars. If there's enough space, it's OK to put out the slides, but restrict your household activity to the inside of the RV.

It is always a good idea to return the casino's hospitality by doing business with them. Treat yourself to a meal in the restaurant, buy something at the gift shop and (the obvious) participate in the gaming if you are so inclined.

We cannot emphasize enough that security personnel must be notified if you plan to stay overnight. Some will ask to see your driver's license or will ask you to complete a form showing your name, vehicle plate and drivers license number along with the date of your visit to the casino.

Even though casinos have 24-hour security, the type of security provided at a large open parking lot is not the same as at an RV park or campground. It is not wise to leave your RV unattended overnight or for any extended period. You would think this advice is just good common sense. But you'd be surprised at how many folks would leave their large expensive vehicles in a casino lot and go off to visit friends in the area for a few days. If you are foolish enough to do this, don't be surprised, when you return, to find your unattended vehicle has been towed away. Many casinos that permit overnight parking limit it to 24 hours and that's as it should be. If you are going to be in the area for more than a day or two, check into an RV park!

Boondocking at a casino is convenient. You have the advantage of having your home with you and you can either walk or take the shuttle bus back and forth to the casino. You can play shorter more relaxing gaming sessions with breaks in between. If you are averse to crowds, you can play at odd hours and avoid peak play times. For couples, when one wants to play cards or slots and the other doesn't, there's no problem. And, of course, there's the obvious benefit – blacktop boondocking is free!

Blacktop Boondocking Etiquette

RVers should never abuse the hospitality of private businesses that allow free overnight parking. The Escapees RV Club has established nine simple rules for proper overnight parking etiquette. FMCA and other national clubs have also adopted the creed as a model for their members as well. Be a considerate blacktop boondocker and observe these rules:

1. Stay one night only.
2. Obtain permission from a qualified individual.
3. Obey posted regulations.
4. No awning, chairs or barbecue grills.
5. Avoid using slideouts.
6. Do not use leveling jacks on slideouts.
7. Purchase gas, food or supplies as a form of thank-you when feasible.
8. Always leave an area cleaner than when you found it.
9. Practice safety precautions.

NOTE:
Many casinos have fee-pay RV parks or campgrounds. (They are listed in the chart on page 259). Some of these casinos will also allow free overnight parking in their parking lot. But others expect you to stay and pay at their RV park and do not permit free overnight parking. If you want to dry camp in the parking lot of a casino that also has an RV park, it's imperative to clear it with Security.

How to be a Savvy Casino Discounter

Casinos are big on promotions. They are continuously offering "specials" and discounts designed to bring you into their facility and onto the gaming floor. Specific discounts are regularly offered at many of the casinos listed in this book.

Senior citizen discounts are among the most common type of discount. Most casinos cater to seniors by offering percent off food or 2-for-1 meals on specific days and some casinos even spring for free breakfast or lunch. The definition of "senior citizen" also varies – some consider 65 and older to qualify for the senior discount while other casinos define senior as 60+ 55+ or 50+. People over 50 should always ask about discounts.

Other frequent discounts are percent off at restaurants and gift shops for Players Club members or weekly specials at the restaurants, such as prime rib night or seafood buffets at special prices. Many casinos give Fun Books, containing valuable coupons.

Casino RV parks will generally extend the same discounts offered at their hotel – AAA and AARP. Most also honor Good Sam and FMCA discounts and some participate in the Escapees or Passport America programs. Seasonally, casino RV parks will run promotions such as one night free if you stay two nights or deeply discounted daily camping fees on the first two or three nights. When you make your reservation or check in, be sure to ask about current discounts. You won't know about some discounts, if you don't ask!

Two important points regarding discounts:

1) Always ask about discounts, current promotions and giveaways! We've discovered that, in many locations, if you don't request the discount (or if you don't know about the discounts), you'll pay full price. Don't be too shy to ask about discounts!

2) Always join the Players Club when you go into a casino, even if you plan to be there only for a few hours. It doesn't cost anything to join and chances are you'll get discounts or other promotional benefits even if you don't gamble there.

Casino Comps Are For Travelers Too

What's a casino comp? "Comp" is a shortened version of "complimentary" and refers to anything the casino gives you for free in return for your playing there. There was a time when casino comps were only available to high rollers – people who spend thousands of dollars at a time. The casino would comp their hotel room, meals, even travel expenses. But nowadays casinos offer comps to virtually everyone who comes there to play.

Just about every casino has a Players Club (known by various names such as Rewards Club, Winners Circle, Total Rewards, Connection Club, Northern Rewards, Magic Money, etc). which allows patrons the opportunity to accumulate points toward comps, free meals, hotel rooms and even cash-back rewards. Players Clubs originally started as Slots Clubs and were designed to give slot machine players (low rollers) an opportunity to get comps formerly offered only to high rollers at the tables.

It doesn't cost anything to join a casino club. There are no dues, but many benefits! Players Clubs are maturing and nowadays many casinos also expect players at the tables to present their club card to accumulate credit toward comps. In casinos where table players are not expected to be club members, a player at the table should always ask about being rated for comps. The casino may add table comps to slot points on the card or will simply extend comps to the player based on his or her table play. If you play both tables and slots, when you join the club, ask if your table comps and slot points will be combined.

Several large casino organizations now have computerized systems that accumulate points from multiple locations on a single player's account. This is good news for travelers. Now you can have one card, one account in which you accumulate points. For the traveling player, points accumulate as you play and they grow as you go. Nationwide cards (as of this writing) include:

- **Connection Card** – from Caesar's Entertainment earns "comp dollars" that can be used as cash to pay for meals, shows and other amenities. Even though Caesar's is now part of the Harrah's organization, the Connection Card Club remains separate from the Total Rewards Club. Cash back slot bonuses are offered to Connection Card players at Las Vegas properties. Connection Card is linked at Caesar's, Bally's, Hilton and some Grand properties. Points redeem for cash within 90 days and for all other comps within 13 months. Points expire if a card has not been used for 13 months, but the account number stays on the database.

- **IsleOne Club** – from Isle of Capri Casinos, Inc., earns points that can be redeemed for cash and comps plus additional IsleMiles rewards. Currently IsleOne is linked at all Isle properties. Points may expire if a card is not used for more than one year.

- **Total Rewards Card** from Harrah's is a tiered card system that allows players to earn base and bonus reward credits that get deposited in the account together and may be used for comps. Base reward points earned in a given calendar year determine the player's status as Gold, Platinum or Diamond member. Currently Total Rewards is linked at all Harrah's properties, but (as noted above) Connection Card remains separate from Total Rewards. Credits expire if the card is not used for six months.

Players Clubs have various point structures. They give gifts, cash, free meals, hotel rooms and more for accumulations of specific amounts of points. Often a Players Card can accumulate enough points in a single session to get a dollar or two or even half off a meal at the casino. When you apply for your card, be sure to find out about the awards structure and ask for the brochure describing point calculations and awards.

When you're playing at the casino, always make sure your card is inserted into the gaming machine before you begin. If the card reader is flashing, try re-inserting the card until the welcome message appears. Points won't accumulate unless the card is properly inserted. For table players, put your card on the table and be sure pit personnel get your information.

Why do casinos like to attach those long colorful bungee cords to their cards? Because slots players are prone to losing the card as they move around the gaming floor. The casino is hoping you'll attach the other end of that cord to yourself. But, if you lose your card while moving around the casino floor, take time to go back to the Club desk and get a duplicate card. Better yet, ask for two cards when you join so you'll have one at the ready should you lose the first card.

Don't think that because you are just passing through for a one or two-day visit to the casino you won't be able to accumulate enough points for comps. When going into a casino for the first time, stop at the Players Club desk and apply for a card. When you do, ask if the casino offers any incentives for new club members. Often they'll give you a free gift just for joining – things like a roll of coins to get you started on the slots, $10 of match play, restaurant meal coupons, free tee shirts, free travel bag or other logo'd items.

Casinos are continuously sponsoring special promotions that, for you, could mean a free gift, a meal coupon, free entry to a slot tournament or an entry to a drawing. Examples of some promotions include senior citizen day once or twice a week, men's and ladies night specials and special drawings. But, you won't know about these promotional comps unless you ask. Most of the time you need to be a Players Club member to participate. Some casinos extend discounts at its restaurants and gift shops for Players Club members.

Points earned on a Players Club card generally expire after one year. So if you're visiting individual casinos in different parts of the country (not linked to a central database), your card is apt to expire by the time you get around to that casino for a second visit. But this could work to your advantage; if the casino drops your name in addition to your points off their database, you can become a new member again, qualifying you for new member promotions if available.

Bottom line: familiarize yourself with club rules and take advantage of all the free "stuff" being offered by casinos.

What's The Difference Between Gaming and Gambling?

Don't go to a casino expecting to win big. Don't expect to make a killing at the table or hit the big jackpot on the slots. Sure it happens, but not for the overwhelming majority of players.

Lots of how-to articles and books have been written about winning at casinos – on topics such as How To Win At Poker, Blackjack Strategies, Winning At Slots, How To Beat The Odds, etc, etc. Advice from professional gamblers may have some merit for other professionals, but this book is designed for casual or recreational casino players.

The average recreational player is by no means a professional gambler. For a casual player, going to the casino should not be about winning or losing…it should be about playing games as a form of entertainment. In this regard we see a difference between gaming and gambling.

As we all learned from the time we first played Monopoly or little league baseball, every game has a winner and a loser. Those who play only to win – and expect to win every time they play – are unrealistic. They put themselves under a lot of stress and take all the fun out of playing games.

Our winning strategy for playing games at the casino is to set limits on money and time and then relax and have fun.

1) **Set a dollar limit and stick to it**. The amount you set – your bankroll – becomes your personal "price of admission" to the casino for that gaming session. If you use up the budgeted bankroll before the end of the session (length of session explained below), stop playing! Come back for another session in a few hours, a few days, weeks, or months – whatever is your style. It is a big mistake to pump more money into an already losing session.

2) **Set a time limit for the gaming session and stick to it**. Always

remember that, no matter what game you play, the odds are in the casino's favor. Longer sessions increase the casino's odds even more. By playing shorter sessions you'll probably keep part or all of your original bankroll longer. If you are winning when your time limit is up, be disciplined enough to end the session as a winner. You still have the original bankroll and won't need to pay your personal pre-set price of admission the next time you come to the casino.

3) **Never ever set your bankroll at more than you can afford to lose!** This simple bit of advice will keep you in the arena of recreational gaming. Keep in mind the odds are always in the casino's favor. Be sensible.

4) **Relax and have fun**. Once you've established the mindset of gaming as entertainment, you can go ahead and have fun at it, knowing you are disciplined enough to spend no more than the specified amount at no longer than the specified time period. Nowadays casinos offer more fun than ever. Slot machines have moved far beyond the boring reels of endless cherries and bars to interactive and entertaining electronic slots. There are machines that replicate popular TV game shows, machines that talk back to you and games that beguile the player with lively, imaginative graphics. And there are machines to accommodate every budget – pennies, nickels, quarters, dollars and even $10, $50 and $100 slots at some locations. Table game fans, too, have more variety. Today there's a wider range of games and, in many places, low minimums for the novice player.

Table players can benefit most from the "specific bankroll and session time" strategy. Disciplined players can relax and enjoy the camaraderie and games at the tables. And, by applying the strategy outlined above, they're more apt to leave a winner.

What does it mean to leave as a winner? A player who leaves with all or part of his bankroll in his pocket is a winner! Players who have the good common sense to leave when they are even or slightly ahead are winners.

For Some, Gambling Is Not An Option

Problem gamblers tell us that winning is easy…leaving is hard. If you can identify with this, read on.

For the large majority of people gambling is fun – it's not a problem. But for some it can become a problem that interferes with their life and literally takes over. If casino gambling is a form of entertainment for you, then you also need to be aware that there is a progressive illness called compulsive gambling.

Gamblers generally fall into three categories:

1. The casual or occasional gambler for whom casino gaming is a form of entertainment.

2. Professional gamblers who have a studied approach to games with an element of skill so that they have an advantage. Their motivation is economic gain. The professional gambler gambles to live; a compulsive gambler lives to gamble.

3. Problem and compulsive gamblers. The problem gambler cannot resist impulses to gamble and is on the way to becoming a compulsive (pathological) gambler. A person is a compulsive gambler if the gambling behavior takes over to the point where it disrupts and damages his or her personal and professional life. That person should seek help.

Gamblers Anonymous is an organization of compulsive gamblers who seek recovery from the illness. GA lists the following 20 questions and notes that if you answer yes to at least seven of them, you may be a problem gambler:

1. Do you lose time from work due to gambling?
2. Does gambling make your home life unhappy?
3. Does gambling affect your reputation?
4. Do you ever feel remorse after gambling?

5. Do you ever gamble to get money to pay debts or otherwise solve financial difficulties?
6. Does gambling cause a decrease in your ambition or efficiency?
7. After losing do you feel you must return as soon as possible to win back your losses?
8. After a win do you have a strong urge to return and win more?
9. Do you often gamble until your last dollar is gone?
10. Do you ever borrow to finance your gambling?
11. Do you ever sell anything to finance your gambling?
12. Are you reluctant to use your gambling money for other expenses?
13. Does gambling make you careless about the welfare of your family?
14. Do you ever gamble longer than you planned?
15. Do you ever gamble to escape worry or trouble?
16. Do you ever commit or consider committing an illegal act to finance your gambling?
17. Does gambling cause you to have difficulty sleeping?
18. Do arguments, disappointments or frustrations create within you an urge to gamble?
19. Do you have an urge to celebrate good fortune by a few hours of gambling?
20. Do you ever consider self-destruction as a result of your gambling?

Compulsive gambling is a diagnosable and treatable illness. It can be as debilitating as drug or alcohol addiction. A 24-hour help line is available at 1-800-522-4700.

Arizona

Four casino resorts in Arizona have full service RV parks. Apache Gold in San Carlos and Hon-Dah in Pinetop are both located on Apache tribal lands in eastern Arizona, easily accessible from US-60. Fort McDowell RV Park is north of Phoenix, just off the Beeline, and Spirit Mountain is on US-95 in northwestern Arizona.

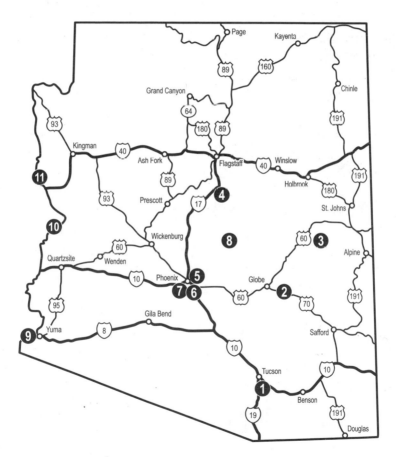

Most other casinos are RV-friendly, that is they have ample and free overnight RV parking. Casino Del Sol and Casino of the Sun are the exceptions as they do not allow overnight parking for self-contained RVs.

Currently 17 Indian Tribes operate casinos in Arizona. Gaming compacts were first negotiated with Arizona's tribes in 1992-93 allowing them to offer slot machines in casinos on tribal lands. In 2003, the compacts were amended to include blackjack and poker table games.

Tucson Area, page 25

Eastern Arizona, page 26

Central Arizona & Phoenix Area, page 28

Western Arizona, page 31

Tuscon Area — Near I-19

Casino Del Sol
5655 West Valencia
Tucson, Arizona 85746 — **Map location #1**
520-883-1700 • 800-344-9435
www.casinodelsol.com

Description: This large gaming complex is owned and operated by the Pascua Yaqui Tribe. The casino has the full complement of pit/table games, slots and a poker room. The open-air ambiance of the casino simulates a town square of a Mediterranean city with Tuscan-style buildings and fountains. Some 50 feet above the gaming floor is a hand-painted ceiling mural of the sky, and special lighting creates a feeling of day and night through vibrant sunrises and sunsets. Six dining options include buffet, fine dining and a California 60's-style diner. The Sunday Brunch is exceptional. The casino is open 24 hours daily. Live entertainment is featured in the outdoor amphitheater.

Directions & Parking: From I-19 exit 95 (W Valencia Rd exit), eight miles west on Valencia. Parking lots have ample space for RVs during the day, but overnight parking is NOT permitted.

Casino of the Sun
7406 South Camino De Oeste
Tucson, Arizona 85746 — **Map location #1**
520-883-1700 • 800-344-9435
www.casinosun.com

Description: A smaller sister casino to Casino Del Sol, it has 500 slots, video poker, video roulette and seven live action blackjack tables plus two restaurants, a smoke shop and gift shop.

Discounts: Ask about current Club Sol promotions and/or senior citizen discounts. Food discounts may be featured on Tuesdays and Thursdays.

Directions & Parking: From I-19 exit 95 (W Valencia Rd exit), seven miles west to Camino De Oeste. Turn left to the casino. There is ample space for RVs in the parking lot during the day, but overnight parking is not permitted.

Desert Diamond: I-19
1100 West Pima Mine Road
Sahuarita, Arizona 85629 — **Map location #1**
520-294-7777 • 866-332-9467
www.desertdiamondcasino.com

Description: Open 24/7, the 15,000 square foot casino has 500 slots, blackjack tables and keno. Food venues include the buffet, a menu service restaurant and a 24-hour café. Casino hours: 9am-4am/24 hrs (Sat-Sun). There is a 2,500-seat event center.

Directions & Parking: From I-19 exit 80, the casino is on the north side of Pima Mine Rd. Free overnight parking for large vehicles is at the north end of the lot; shuttle service is available to the casino.

Eastern Arizona

Apache Gold Casino Resort & RV Park
Box 1210
San Carlos, AZ 85550 — **Map Location #2**
928-475-7800 • 800-APACHE 8
928-475-7800 Ext. 3201 (RV park)
www.apachegoldcasinoresort.com

Description: The fully paved RV park has 60 extra wide pull-thru sites with water, electric, sewer and CATV. All sites are walking distance to the casino. The mountain view park also has a heated pool and spa, laundry room and convenience store. The 2005 rate was $12 per night. There is a hotel with 146 rooms and live entertainment is featured nightly in the Cabaret. Apache Gold has the #1 public golf course in Arizona, and there is excellent bass fishing nearby. The 24-hour casino has more than 500 slots, video poker, keno, blackjack tables and a live action poker room. There is a buffet restaurant and the Apache grill.

Discounts: Good Sam discount is given at the RV park. Also ask about seasonal promotions for RV park guests.

Directions: From Jct. US-70 & US-60 in Globe, go east for six miles on US-70 (a major four-lane road). RV parking is also permitted in the casino lot.

Hon-Dah Casino Resort & RV Park
777 Highway 260
Pinetop, AZ 85935 — **Map Location #3**
928-369-0299 • 800-929-8744
928-369-7400 (RV park)
www.hon-dah.com

Description: The resort is located in the White Mountains of eastern Arizona. The RV park features 258 level wooded sites (80 are pull-thrus) in a pine forest. All sites have patios, full hookups plus CATV and phone connections at each site. The park has a gas station and convenience store and is open all year. Summer is the busy season and reservations are suggested since most sites are seasonally occupied. Daily RV rate in 2005 was $23, with weekly and monthly rates available. The RV park is across the street from the casino and within walking distance from most sites. The casino has over 600 slots plus six gaming tables, poker room, two restaurants, a cigar bar and gift shop. The poker room opens every day at 4 pm. The hotel has 200 rooms.

Discounts: Good Sam discount is honored at the RV park. New Players Club members receive a Fun Book.

Directions & Parking: Located at Jct. Hwy-260 & Hwy-73 (three miles south of Pinetop). From I-40 exit 286, take Hwy-77 south for 47 miles to Show Low, then US-60/77 south to Hwy-260 east for 15.5 miles to the casino resort. You may park in the casino lot if staying for a few hours, but if you plan an overnight stay please check in to the RV Park.

Central Arizona & Phoenix Area

Cliff Castle Casino
555 Middle Verde Road — **Map Location #4**
Camp Verde, Arizona 86322
928-567-7900 • 800-381-SLOT
www.cliffcastle.com

Description: Open every day 24 hours, the 14,000 square foot casino is located in Cliff Castle Lodge about 50 miles south of Flagstaff. The casino features 570 slots, eight gaming tables, poker room and five restaurants. The lodge has 84 rooms. There is a bowling alley on property. Outdoor concerts are held in the Stargazer Pavilion.

Directions & Parking: From I-17 exit 289, the casino is about one mile east of the interstate (follow signs). RV parking is in the lower lot; overnight parking is permitted. However, the casino building is some distance up a rather steep hill and shuttle service is sporadic. You may need to phone for the shuttle.

Fort McDowell Casino & RV Park
10424 North Fort McDowell Road
Fountain Hills, AZ 85264 — **Map Location #5**
480-837-1424 • 800-THE-FORT
480-836-5310 (RV park)
www.fortmcdowellcasino.com

Description: Open 24 hours daily, the casino has 775 slot machines (reel, video and progressives), live keno and bingo seven days a week. There is 24-hour blackjack and poker in the card room with 24-hour tableside food service. A modern 200 full-hookup site RV park is located just across the street from the casino building. Last year's daily rate was from $32. There are also phone hookups at the sites. On-site food venues include Silver Platter in the bingo hall, Café 87 for Asian and American dining, Beeline Deli, Verde River Buffet, The Peaks Steakhouse and food and drink specials in Lucky 7 Saloon.

Discounts: A Player's Club discount is given at restaurants.

Directions & Parking: From State Road 87 north (the Beeline), exit at Fort McDowell Road (approximately 25 miles north of Phoenix). If staying overnight, RVs are required to check into the RV park.

Gila River Casinos
1200 South 56th Street (Lone Butte)
5512 West Wild Horse Pass (Wild Horse)
Chandler, Arizona 85226 — **Map Location #6**
520-796-7777 • 800-WIN-GILA
www.wingilariver.com

Description: Two separate casino buildings are both located next to I-10 at exit 162. The Lone Butte facility can be seen from the northbound lanes of the interstate. It has 600 slots, 27 blackjack tables, video poker and video keno. The Wild Horse casino, near the southbound lanes, has 750 slots, keno, live poker and blackjack, a 1,500-seat high-stakes bingo hall, buffet restaurant, two delis and a gift shop. Both are open 24/7.

Directions & Parking: From I-10, exit 162: *To Wildhorse* go west on Wild Horse Pass Blvd., then south on 48th St., then west on Wild Horse Pass Rd., or *To Lone Butte*: go west on Stardust Rd., then north on 56th St. Ample RV parking is available at both locations. The casino requests that Security be notified if you plan to stay overnight. Please observe a two-day stay limit.

Harrah's Ak-Chin Resort Casino
15406 Maricopa Road
Maricopa, Arizona 85239 — **Map Location #7**
480-802-5000 • 800-HARRAHS
www.harrahs.com

Description: Open 24/7, the 43,000 square-foot casino features 850 slots (denominations from 1¢ up), keno parlor, 12 blackjack tables, poker room and bingo. The resort has a 146-room/suite hotel, four restaurants, a Native American crafts shop and a smoke shop. Free entertainment is featured in the Oasis Lounge.

Discounts: Various senior discounts are offered; Total Rewards cardholders receive buffet discounts.

Directions & Parking: From I-10 exit 164, turn right on to Queen Creek Road for 17 miles to the casino. After entering the Ak-Chin property, go to the large parking area to the left, designated for large vehicles. Overnight parking is permitted.

Mazatzal Casino
Highway 87 at Milepost 251
Payson, Arizona 85547 — **Map Location #8**
928-474-6044 • 800-777-7529
www.777play.com

Description: Open daily 24 hours, the casino features 390 slots in all denominations including many 1¢ and 2¢ machines. The card room, open daily from 10am-1am has live action blackjack tables with 4-deck shoes and liberal rules and poker with a "Bad Beat Jackpot" on Texas Hold 'Em.

Discounts: Ask about Fun Books for discounts.

Directions & Parking: The casino is about 90 miles northeast of Phoenix. Go north on US Hwy-87 (the Beeline) to mile marker 251. Follow signs to overflow parking and park on the level lots across from the casino. The casino is walking distance from all parking areas. Check with Security if you plan to stay overnight.

Note: RVs should avoid the parking lot at the front of the casino – steep grades going into that lot are not for motor homes; you could bottom out.

Western Arizona

Cocopah Casino
15136 South Avenue B (Rt-95)
Somerton, Arizona 85350 — **Map Location #9**
928-726-8066 • 800-23-SLOTS
www.wincocopahcasino.com

Description: The renovated and expanded casino includes 475 slots, eight blackjack tables and two sessions daily in the 250-seat bingo hall. The Artisan Restaurant has buffet and menu service.

Discounts: Ask at the Players Club about seasonal senior discounts.

Directions & Parking: From I-8 near the California border, exit at 16th St. Take 16th St. to Avenue B (US-95). Go seven miles south on Avenue B toward Somerton. There are 30 spaces designated for RV parking; overnight is OK.

Paradise Casino
450 Quechan Dive
Yuma, Arizona 85364 — **Map Location #9**
760-572-7777 • 888-777-4946
www.paradise-casinos.com

Description: Paradise has two separate casino buildings – one on the Arizona side and one on the California side of the state line. They are within walking distance of each other. The Arizona casino has 675 slots (no gaming tables) and a restaurant. The California casino has 200 slots plus poker room and blackjack tables (no restaurant).

Discounts: Free breakfast is given with three hours of rated blackjack play. Club Paradise cardholders get 10% off at the restaurant.

Directions & Parking: From I-8 exit at 4th Ave. Follow the casino signs. RVs may park anywhere on the dirt area designated for large vehicles. Overnight parking is permitted for persons in the casino.

Blue Water Casino
119 West Riverside Drive
Parker, Arizona 85344 — **Map Location #10**
928-669-7777 • 888-243-3366
www.bluewaterfun.com

Description: The 24-hour casino features 460 slots, live keno and live action poker and blackjack. Food venues include the buffet and fine dining. There is a 225-room/suite hotel. The resort is located on the Colorado River.

Directions & Parking: Located 160 miles west of Phoenix, from I-10 exit at US-95, north for about 45 miles into Parker. Turn right at Riverside Drive and go 1.5 miles to the casino. Designated RV parking is in the upper lot. Overnight RV stays are limited to one night.

Spirit Mountain Casino & RV Park
8555 South Highway 95
Mohave Valley, Arizona 86440 — **Map Location #11**
928-346-2000 • 928-346-1225 (RV park)

Description: The 120-space RV park has full hookups on level sites in an open desert setting. Big rigs are welcome. 2005 daily rates were $17 and weekly and monthly rates are available. Cable TV and phone hookups are available (on arrival); laundry and dump station. The RV park is open all year. It is located adjacent to a cozy casino that has 180 slots, video poker and keno (no table games).

Directions: From I-40 exit 1, take US-95 north for 12 miles into Mohave Valley. The casino is located on the southbound side of US-95.

California

Gaming came to the state in March 2000, when Californians passed Proposition 1A which called for the state to effect compacts with Indian tribal leaders aimed at permitting casinos on California's Indian lands. The legislation was challenged but upheld by the courts. California currently has more gaming tribes than any other state with 43 hosting some form of gambling. Indian gaming continues to be a significant political issue.

Although most Indian casinos don't have RV parks, they are generally RV-friendly and allow free overnight parking for self-contained vehicles. Some casinos are in mountainous locations; steep grades are identified in directions to these facilities. Casinos that are too small, too remote or difficult for RVs to access are not included in this book. Casinos that do not permit RV

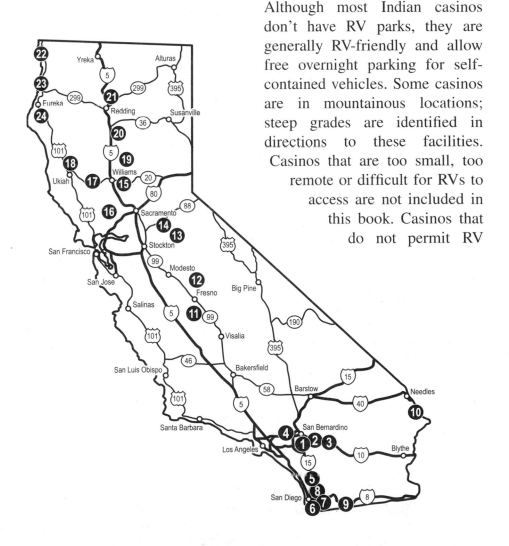

parking are likewise excluded. RV travelers in Central California should be aware that the Thunder Valley Casino in Lincoln, CA (northeast of Sacramento) does NOT permit RVs on their property.

Casino RV parks in California include: Pechanga Casino (east of Los Angeles), Konocti Vista Casino (north of San Francisco), Feather Falls Casino (north of Sacramento) and Lake Havasu (near the Arizona state line).

Southern California, page 35

Map	Casino
1	Pechanga Resort and Casino & RV Park
2	Agua Caliente Casino
2	Morongo Casino Resort
2	Soboba Casino
3	Augustine Casino
3	Fantasy Springs Casino
3	Trump 29
4	San Manuel Indian Bingo & Casino
5	Pala Casino
5	Casino Pauma
5	Harrah's Rincon Casino & Resort
5	Valley View Casino
6	Sycuan Casino
7	Viejas Casino
8	Barona Valley Ranch Resort and Casino
9	Golden Acorn Casino
10	Havasu Landing Resort, Casino & RV Park

Central California, page 44

Map	Casino
11	Palace Indian Gaming Center
12	Chukchansi Gold Resort & Casino
12	Table Mountain Casino & Bingo
13	Black Oak Casino at Tuolumne Rancheria

Northern California, page 51

Southern California

Pechanga Resort and Casino & RV Park
45000 Pechanga Parkway
Temecula, California 92592 — **Map Location #1**
909-693-1819 • 877-711-2WIN
877-99RVFUN (RV park)
www.pechanga.com

Description: The resort includes a hotel with 522 rooms/suites and an RV park with 170 sites. The modern, full service RV park has a heated pool, two Jacuzzi spas, recreation room in the clubhouse, laundry, gas station, car wash and convenience store. The park can serve as a home base for visitors exploring southern California. Last year's RV rates: $32 per night. Reservations are suggested. Shuttle service is provided to the

24-hour casino that has 2,000 slots, 126 gaming tables, high stakes room and a 54-table non-smoking poker room with daily tournaments. There are six restaurants and live entertainment is featured at the casino.

Discounts: The RV park honors Good Sam, AAA and AARP discounts.

Directions: From I-15 Indio/Route 79 South exit, (Pechanga Indian Reservation signs at exit). south on Route 79 for .7 mile, right on Pechanga Parkway for 1.5 miles to the resort complex.

Agua Caliente Casino
32250 Bob Hope Drive
Rancho Mirage, CA 92270 — **Map Location #2**
760-321-2000 • 866-858-3600
www.hotwatercasino.com

Description: Owned and operated by the Agua Caliente Band of Cahuilla Indians, this modern casino has 1,100 slots, 46 gaming tables, high limit gaming area, six restaurants, cabaret-style lounge and video poker bar. The casino floor has both smoking and non-smoking areas.

Discounts: On weekdays Players Club members get the breakfast buffet for buy one and get the second for 50% off.

Directions & Parking: From I-10 at Ramon Rd exit, the casino is next to the westbound lanes of the interstate. RVs are invited to park at Flying J, just across the interstate from the casino (I-10 Ramon exit). The casino has a parking arrangement with Flying J. There is a casino courtesy phone at the J Store. Call for a pickup. A casino valet will provide transportation to and from your rig.

Morongo Casino Resort
49750 Seminole Drive
Cabazon, California 92230 — **Map Location #2**
951-849-3080 • 800-252-4499
www.casinomorongo.com

Description: The 150,000 square foot casino located 90 miles east of Los Angeles has 2,000 slots, 50 blackjack tables and a 22-table poker room. Dining choices include Potrero Canyon Buffet, Serrano Restaurant, Sunset Bar & Grill, The Steakhouse and a food court. There is a 310-room hotel on site.

Discounts: Winners Club members receive 10% off at the gift shop.

Directions & Parking: From I-10 at the Cabazon exit, the casino can be seen from the interstate. RVs should use the northeast area of the parking lot; follow signs for RV/truck parking. Call the casino for the shuttle. Overnight parking is permitted.

Soboba Casino
23333 Soboba Road
San Jacinto, California 92583 — **Map Location #2**
951-654-2883 • 866-4-SOBOBA
www.soboba.net

Description: The 24-hour casino has over 2,000 slots, table games and a poker room open 24/7. Restaurants include Café Soboba, Steakhouse and Spicy Sushi & Teriyaki. Live entertainment is featured on weekends.

Discounts: The steakhouse extends discounts to Players Club members. Also, ask about weekly Player Appreciation Days.

Directions & Parking: Located 90 miles east of Los Angeles, from I-215 exit 22 take the Ramona Freeway for 30 miles to Lake Park Dr. Turn left to the stop sign, then right on Soboba Rd. for about a mile to the casino. RVs should park toward the back of the lot. Overnight parking is OK.

Augustine Casino
84001 Avenue 54
Coachella, CA 92236 — **Map Location #3**
760-391-9500 • 888-752-9204
www.augustinecasino.com

Description: This cozy 24/7 casino is located about five miles from Interstate 10; it has a variety of coinless slots, a dozen gaming tables and The Patio Restaurant and Café 54 (open 24 hours).

Directions & Parking: From 1-10, Hwy-86/Dillon Road exit, south on Dillon Road for 1.5 miles and south on Van Buren Street for three miles to the casino (corner of Van Buren & Avenue 54). RVs should park on the east side of the lot.

Fantasy Springs Casino
84-245 Indio Springs Drive
Indio, California 92203 — **Map Location #3**
760-342-5000 • 800-827-2WIN
www.fantasyspringsresort.com

Description: The 24/7 casino located in the Palm Springs Valley, has 1,900 slots, 30 gaming tables (liberal blackjack rules) and a separate 8-table poker room with daily tournaments. Off track betting is featured in the Triple Crown Room. Bingo is called every day. Food venues include: Players Steakhouse, Fantasy Café (open 24 hours), Fresh Grill Buffet, The Bistro and two lounges. Fantasy Lanes Bowling has 24 lanes.

Discounts: Club Fantasy members get a discount on Sunday brunch.

Directions & Parking: Located 125 miles east of Los Angeles, exit I-10 at Golf Center Parkway. The casino is visible from the interstate. RV parking is behind the hotel. Overnight parking is permitted.

Trump 29
46-200 Harrison Place
Coachella, California 92236 — **Map Location #3**
760-775-5566 • 866-TRUMP29
www.trump29.com

Description: Owned by the 29 Palms Band of Indians, the 75,000 square-foot casino is open daily 24 hours. It has 2,000 slots, 35 gaming tables, a poker room, two restaurants and a fast food court. Headline entertainment is featured in the 2,500-seat showroom.

Directions & Parking: From I-10 Dillon exit (130 miles east of Los Angeles), the casino can be seen from the eastbound lanes of the interstate. RV parking is next to the truck parking. Overnight is OK, but stays are limited to 24 hours.

San Manuel Indian Bingo & Casino
5797 North Victoria Avenue
Highland, California 92346 — **Map Location #4**
909-864-5050 • 800-359-2464
www.sanmanuel.com

Description: The 24-hour casino has 2,000 ticket-in/ticket-out slots, blackjack and three-card poker tables and open play and daily jackpots in the poker room. Bingo is held every day except Thursday. Free entertainment is featured nightly in the Tukut Lounge. Food is available at the Serrano Buffet, Sports Watch Grill and the food court. There is live headline entertainment on weekends.

Directions & Parking: From I-10 take the 30 Freeway east (to 330); exit right at Highland Ave, turn left to Victoria and stay on Victoria to the casino. Continue up the hill to Lots 2 & 3, designated for RVs. Security is on site and will assist with parking. Shuttle service is available 24 hours.

Pala Casino
11154 Highway 76
Pala, California 92054 — **Map Location #5**
760-510-5100 • 877-946-7252
www.palacasino.com

Description: The Vegas-style resort has a 507-room/suite hotel, fitness center and spa, casino with 2,250 slots, 85 gaming tables, two lounges and eight restaurants, including a buffet, café, Noodles, a steakhouse and more. It is open 24/7. Headline entertainment appears at the 2000-seat Pala Events Center and the Palomar Starlight Theater.

Directions & Parking: Located 35 miles northeast of San Diego, from I-15 exit at SR-76 (Pala/Oceanside). Take SR-76 east for five miles to the casino. RVs should park in the west lot, within walking distance to the casino. RV parking is limited to 24 hours.

Casino Pauma
777 Pauma Reservation Road
Pauma Valley, California 92061 — **Map Location #5**
760-742-2177 • 877-687-2862
www.casinopauma.com

Description: The 24-hour casino has Vegas style gaming – slots from 1¢ to $5 and table pit/games including pai gow, craps and roulette; $2 blackjack tables Mon–Fri except holidays and $3 blackjack on Thursdays. The poker room has tournaments on weekends. Restaurants include the Pauma Bay Café and buffet. Outdoor dining is available under the covered patio overlooking the Palamar Mountains.

Discounts: Senior lunch buffets, 1–4pm every day, are 50% off. Breakfast specials are 95¢. All-you-can-eat prime ribs are on Fridays and Saturdays.

Directions & Parking: Located 35 miles northeast of San Diego. Take I-15 to Hwy-76 (Oceanside/Pala exit) east (road has steep grades) for 12 miles to Pauma Reservation Rd. (Street sign is partially obstructed. Look for Jilburto's Taco Shop on the right and get into the left lane.) Turn left on to Pauma Reservation Rd. for a half mile to the casino. Free parking is available for RVs. Turn right at the casino, then take the first right into the parking lot – walking distance to the casino.

Harrah's Rincon Casino & Resort
33750 Valley Center Road
Valley Center, CA 92082 — **Map Location #5**

760-751-3100 • 877-777-2457
www.harrahs.com

Description: The Vegas-style resort casino features 1,600 slots and video poker and over 40 table games. Among the slots is the volcanic bingo roulette, a creative alternative to the traditional game of roulette. Six food venues include the signature International Buffet, San Luis Rey Café, Fiore Steakhouse, Oyster Bar and Fortune's Asian. There is a coffee bar and casual grill. Live entertainment is featured in the Oasis Bar. The hotel has 651 rooms/suites. Concerts are held in the Open Sky Theater.

Discounts: Total Rewards cardholders receive a $5 discount at the Friday Lobster buffet. Cardholders also get discounts at the gift shop.

Directions & Parking: Located ten miles north of Escondido, from I-15 exit at Valley Parkway going east. Valley Parkway turns into Valley Center Rd. (You will travel several miles through Escondido before the street changes to Valley Center Rd.) Follow Valley Center Rd for about eight miles to Harrah's on the left. RVs should park behind the casino building. Overnight is OK.

Valley View Casino
16300 Nyemii Pass Road
Valley Center, California 92082 — **Map Location #5**
760-291-5500 • 866-726-7277
www.valleyviewcasino.com

Description: The 24-hour casino has 900 slots in all denominations and 12 gaming tables. Food venues include the Market Square Steak & Seafood Buffet and Café de View (open 24 hrs).

Discounts: VIP Players Club members get $2 off the buffet.

Directions: From I-15 take the Escondido exit at Valley Pkwy, then east on Valley Pkwy for five miles – it becomes Valley Center Rd. Follow signs to the casino. RVs should park on Level 3 (second driveway past the main entrance). Shuttle service is provided to the casino.

Sycuan Casino
5469 Casino Way
El Cajon, California 92019 — **Map Location #6**
619-445-6002 • 800-279-2826
www.sycuancasino.com

Description: Ten miles east of San Diego, the two-story, 73,000 square foot casino has 2,000 slots, 28 tables. Restaurants include the Washina Falls Café and Oasis Buffet in the casino. The Sunset Deli is open 24 hours and there is a snack bar in the bingo hall. There is a 103-room lodge with golf and tennis in the resort. Live entertainment is featured in the Showcase Theater.

Discounts: Senior Day on Wednesday features breakfast, $5 match play and 50% off the buffet.

Directions & Parking: From I-8 El Cajon Second St exit, south on Second and left on Washington for one mile. The street name changes to Dehesa, proceed for six more miles to the casino. RVs should park in the overflow lot – walking distance to the casino.

Viejas Casino
5000 Willows Road
Alpine, California 91901 — **Map Location #7**
619-445-5400 • 800-84POKER
www.viejas.com

Description: Located 25 miles east of San Diego, the casino features 2,000 slots, gaming tables, poker room and bingo. Food venues include Grove Steakhouse, Harvest Buffet, Sunrise Diner, China Camp and the Deli. Headline entertainment appears at concerts in the park.

Directions & Parking: From I-8 exit (Alpine Blvd/Willows Rd) take

Willows Road north for 1.5 miles. The paved lot on the east side is designated for large vehicles. It is walking distance to the casino.

Barona Valley Ranch Resort and Casino
1932 Wildcat Canyon Road
Lakeside, California 92040 — **Map Location #8**
619-443-2300 • 888-7-BARONA
www.barona.com

Description: Owned and operated by the Barona Band of Mission Indians, the casino features 2,000 slots, video poker, video roulette, modified craps and 59 live table games. There is a poker room, off track betting parlor and bingo hall. The resort has a 397-room/suite hotel, four restaurants (including the 850-seat Ranch House Buffet overlooking the golf course), a food court and the Baron Creek Golf Club.

Discounts: Buffet discounts are given for slot club members.

Directions & Parking: Located 15 miles northeast of San Diego. From I-8 take CA-67 north and follow the freeway until it ends at the light in Lakeside; go to the next light and turn right on to Willow Rd for one mile to a four-way stop. Turn left on to Wildcat Canyon Rd for 5.5 miles to the casino. Security will assist with parking.

Golden Acorn Casino
1800 Golden Acorn Way
Campo, California 91906 — **Map Location #9**
619-938-6000 • 866-794-6244
www.goldenacorncasino.com

Description: Located 40 miles east of San Diego, the facility includes a truck stop, convenience store and the Golden Grill Restaurant, open 24 hours with breakfast served anytime. The casino has 750 slots and 12 gaming tables, including blackjack (some $2 tables) and three-card poker.

Discounts: A Fun Book is given with Slot Club signup. Senior discounts (age 55 and older) are given on Tuesdays and Thursdays.

Directions & Parking: At the I-8 Campo exit (25 miles east of Alpine), the casino is visible from the interstate; follow signs. Lots of parking spaces are provided for large vehicles. RVs should park next to the large Golden Acorn sign. Overnight is OK for self-contained vehicles.

Havasu Landing Resort, Casino & RV Park
5 Main Street
Havasu Lake, California 92363 — **Map Location #10**
760-858-4593 • 800-307-3610
www.havasulanding.com

Description: Located on the western shores of Lake Havasu, near the Arizona state line, the resort includes a full-service RV park, mobile homes on the lake and a marina with boat slips. A market, deli and general store are on site. 2005 RV rates are from $10 ($15 waterfront). Weekly, monthly and special holiday package rates are also available. The casino has 220 slots plus live blackjack and poker. Casino hours are 9:30am–12:30am, daily\2:30am (Fri–Sat). Recreational activities include boating, water skiing, boating, swimming, fishing, hunting, jet skiing, windsurfing and sightseeing.

Directions: From I-40 exit 144 at Needles, take US-95 south for 19 miles and turn left at Havasu Lake Rd —or— From I-10 exit 232 at Blythe, take US-95 north for 79 miles and turn right at Havasu Lake Rd.

Central California

Palace Indian Gaming Center
17225 Jersey Avenue
Lemoore, California 93245 — **Map Location #11**
559-924-7751 • 800-942-6886
www.thepalace.net

Description: Open 24 hours daily, the 105,000 square foot casino has five floors of slots, pit/table games, poker room, bingo every day and four restaurants. Live entertainment on weekends.

Directions & Parking: From the 99 Freeway, take Freeway 198 west to 18th Ave in Lemoore, then south on 18th Ave for four miles to Jersey Ave, then left to the casino. RVs should use the dirt lot at the front of the casino. Overnight parking is permitted.

Chukchansi Gold Resort & Casino
711 Lucky Lane
Coarsegold, CA 93614 — **Map Location #12**
559-692-5200 • 866-7-WIN-WIN
www.chukchansigold.com

Description: The casino has 1,800 slots and 47 tables with blackjack, poker and volcanic roulette. Seven themed restaurants include the California buffet, a steakhouse, diner, oriental food, a café and bakery. Live entertainment and large screen TVs are in the Firehouse Blues lounge.

Discounts: Ask about senior citizen specials at the buffet.

Directions & Parking: The casino is located 35 miles north of Fresno. Take Hwy-41 north from Fresno into Coarsegold. From the highway, go up the hill toward the casino and take the first right turn into the parking area for large vehicles. Check in with Security if you plan to stay overnight.

Table Mountain Casino & Bingo
8184 Table Mountain Road
Friant, California 93626 — **Map Location #12**
559-822-2485 • 800-541-3637
www.tmcasino.com

Description: The 24-hour casino features 1,700 slots, 29 tables of blackjack (liberal rules), Let It Ride and three-card poker and a separate nine-table poker room. The Mountain Feast Buffet is open weekdays 11am–9pm/10pm (Fri-Sat). The Eagles Landing restaurant has menu service and Asian specialties. The Trading Post shop features authentic Native American collectibles art work and crafts.

Discounts: Seniors get lunch for $3.99, 11am–4pm Thursdays, with slot card.

Directions & Parking: From Fresno take CA-41 north to Friant Rd. Turn right on Friant Rd for 15 miles, then left on Sky Harbor Rd. RVs should park in the lot on Sky Harbor Rd. Check in with Security if you plan to stay overnight.

Black Oak Casino at Tuolumne Rancheria
19400 Tuolumne Road North
Tuolumne, California 95379 — **Map Location #13**
209-928-9300 • 877-747-8777
www.blackoakcasino.com

Description: The 24/7 casino has 1,000 slots in denominations from pennies to $5, video poker and keno plus 24 gaming tables with blackjack, three and four-card poker and weekly tournaments. There is a non-smoking slots section. It has a 24-hour café, a buffet restaurant and fine dining at Seven Sisters Wed–Sun evenings.

Discounts: $3.99 senior breakfast every Wednesday from 7–11am. Other special senior activities on Wednesdays include slot tournaments.

Directions & Parking: Located in the Sierra foothills, the casino is 100 miles southeast of Sacramento. From Hwy-99 south, exit at Hwy-120 east to Oakdale. Turn left on to Hwy-108 to Somora. Turn right on Tuolumne Rd (second light) and follow signs for eight miles to the casino. Check in with Security if you plan to stay overnight.

Jackson Rancheria Casino & Hotel
12222 New York Ranch Road
Jackson, California 95642 — **Map Location #14**
209-223-1677 • 800-822-WINN
www.jacksoncasino.com

Description: Located 60 miles southeast of Sacramento on the Miwuk Reservation, the 24-hour casino has 1,500 slots, 40 gaming tables, seven-table poker room and bingo on weekends. Dining options include the buffet, two restaurants with menu service and a food court. Free live music is featured in the cabaret. The resort includes a 103-room/suite hotel. Headline entertainment in concert on weekends.

Discounts: 10% off the buffet if 55 and older.

Directions & Parking: From the 99 Freeway in Stockton, take Waterloo Road east, then CA-88 (steep grades) for about 30 miles, then north on Ridge Road for seven miles to New York Ranch Road. After entering the casino property, park in the first lot on the right. Shuttle service is available. Overnight parking is permitted for self-contained vehicles.

Colusa Casino
3770 Highway 45
Colusa, California 95926 — **Map Location #15**
530-458-8844 • 800-655-UWIN
www.colusacasino.com

Description: Located 75 miles north of Sacramento on the Wintun Reservation, the casino has over 750 slots, 12 pit/gaming tables and a separate poker room. Food venues include the buffet and a steakhouse for fine dining. It is open 24/7. There is a 60-room hotel on site

Discounts: Senior Days are held every Tuesday and Sunday. From 8am–8pm seniors (50 and older) receive free $5 slot play and free coffee and pastries; the senior slot tournament is held at 10am.

Directions & Parking: From I-5 Williams exit, east on Hwy-20 for nine miles, north on Hwy-45 for three miles. RVs should park in the lot north of the casino. Overnight is OK.

Cache Creek Indian Bingo & Casino
14455 Highway 16
Brooks, CA 95606 — **Map Location #16**
530-796-3118 • 800-452-8181 (CA) • 800-992-8686
www.cachecreek.com

Description: The casino has 2,000 slots, in all denominations, 120 tables, separate high limit area for blackjack and baccarat players, non-smoking slots area and bingo daily. Blackjack minimum is $5 with maximums to $2,000; high limit jackpots on Caribbean poker. There is a 200-room hotel and health spa, mini mart and gas station. Dining options include a noodle house, fine dining, buffet, 24-hour café, food court and deli.

Discounts: Cash Club play is tracked at slots and tables. New members get a free pull for a $1 million jackpot.

Directions & Parking: The casino is 35 miles northwest of Sacramento. From I-5 in Woodland exit at Esparto/Highway 16. Turn left at the stop sign, go three miles to the stop light at Main St in Woodland. Turn right on Hwy-16 and follow Hwy-16 over the 505 Freeway and through Esparto and Capay. The casino is on the right in Brooks. Ample parking is available for RVs. Overnight is OK.

Twin Pine Casino
22223 Hwy-29 at Rancheria Road
Middletown, California 95461— **Map Location #16**
707-987-0197 • 800-564-4872
www.twinpine.com

Description: The 24/7 casino has 400 slots, blackjack, pai-gow poker, a separate poker room and a café. Entertainment and weekly events are featured.

Directions & Parking: From I-5 in Williams, take Hwy-20 to Hwy-53 toward Clearlake. Stay on Hwy-53 to Lower Lake. At this point you are on Hwy-29. Stay on Hwy-29 through Middletown to the casino about one mile on the right. Free overnight parking is available for RVs.

Konocti Vista Casino & RV Park
2755 Mission Rancheria Road
Lakeport, California 95453 — **Map Location #17**
707-262-1900 • 800-FUN-1950
www.kvcasino.com

Description: Located on Clear Lake, California's largest natural lake, the resort includes a hotel with 80 rooms and a modern RV park. There are 74 paved full hookup sites, CATV, phone service at the sites, showers and a laundry facility at the RV park. Last year's daily RV rate was $30; RVs should register at the hotel. RV guests are invited to use the pool and other hotel amenities. There is a 94-slip marina/boat launch and fishing off the dock. The 24-hour casino features 650 slots, video poker and eight tables. A full service diner is open 6am–10pm.

Discounts: The RV park honors Good Sam, Escapees and Passport America discounts. Senior citizen discount at the diner is 10%. Friday is Senior Day and Sunday is Senior Night at the casino, when $10 match play is offered for seniors 55 and older. Also ask about seasonal discounts and promotions.

Directions & Parking: Located 120 miles north of San Francisco. From US-101, exit 555B take Hwy-20 east for 19 miles, then south on Hwy-29 for 11 miles. Right after Hwy-29 narrows to two lanes, follow Soda Bay Rd signs and turn left at the traffic lights. Go one block and turn right at the stop sign. Travel 1.8 miles on Soda Bay Rd, then turn left onto Mission Rancheria Rd. Boondocking is allowed on the gravel area next to the casino parking lot, but it is limited to two nights. If staying longer, please check into the RV park.

Robinson Rancheria Casino
1545 Highway 20
Nice, California 95464— **Map Location #17**
707-275-9000 • 800-809-3636
www.robinsonrancheria.biz

Description: The 24-hour casino has 600 slots, video poker, progressives, blackjack and Let-It-Ride tables, poker room and 1,000-seat bingo hall. There is a 48-room hotel and conference center, Rancheria Grill, Snack Shack and sports bar. Live entertainment is featured in the showroom. Starbuck's coffee is available in the gift shop. The Aurora RV Park and Marina, also owned by the Poma Indians, is located 2.4 miles east of the casino on Hwy-20. Robinson Rancheria is on the north shore of Clear Lake where there is good fishing.

Discounts: RV guests receive $10 video/slot play at the casino. Ask about senior citizen discounts.

Directions & Parking: Take Hwy-101 north to Ukiah, then CA-20 east toward Upper Lake/Williams. Robinson Rancheria is on the left as you enter Nice. Free overnight parking for RVs is permitted in the casino lot for one night only.

Hopland Sho-Ka-Wah Casino
13101 Nakomis Road
Hopland, California 95449 — **Map Location #17**
707-744-1395 • 888-746-5292
www.shokawah.com

Description: The casino features 1,200 slots, 16 gaming tables, Players Steakhouse and a deli. Casino hours are 9am–10pm/midnight (Thu–Sat).

Directions & Parking: Hopland is 107 miles north of the Golden Gate Bridge. Take US-101 into Hopland, then east on CA-175 for 3.5 miles to the casino. (Exxon station at the corner of the 101 and Hwy-175.)

Note: narrow roads going into the casino. Upon arrival on casino property, check with Security and they will direct you to the parking area for large vehicles. Overnight parking is permitted.

Coyote Valley Casino
7751 North State Street
Redwood Valley, California 95470— **Map Location #18**
707-485-0700 • 800-332-9683
www.coyotevalleycasino.com

Description: The 24-hour casino has 400 slots, video poker, video keno, blackjack and high stakes bingo. Food is available at Angelina's Café.

Directions & Parking: Take the 101 to seven miles north of Ukiah and exit at West Rd to the casino. Free overnight parking is available.

Northern California

Feather Falls Casino & RV Park
3 Alverda Drive
Oroville, California 95966 — **Map Location #19**
530-533-3885 • 866-785-9626
www.featherfallscasino.com

Description: A lighted and paved KOA RV park features 43 full hookup spaces, laundry, Internet service, pet friendly and shuttle service to the casino. Open 24 hours, the casino has 1,000 slots, 11 single deck blackjack tables, a separate 12-table poker room, Dreamcatcher Buffet and Village café serving breakfast, lunch and dinner. Live entertainment is featured on weekends in the 900-seat Cascade Showroom.

Directions & Parking: Located 100 miles north of Sacramento. From Marysville, take CA-70 north for 22.7 miles to Ophir Rd, then three miles east on Ophir Road. Security will assist with parking.

Gold Country Casino
4020 Olive Highway
Oroville, California 95966 — **Map Location #19**
530-538-4560 • 800-334-9400
www.gold-country-casino.com

Description: Owned and operated by the Tyne Maidu Tribe of the Berry Creek Rancheria, the resort has an 87-room hotel and convention center. The 24-hour casino has 700 slots, 14 gaming tables and a poker room open seven days. Dining options include fine dining, a buffet and a 24-hour café.

Discounts: Senior Days on Tuesday and Thursday 7–11am feature free coffee and donuts and $5 voucher for $1 play. Cash Club members get cash back based on their play.

Directions & Parking: From Marysville, CA-70 north to Oroville. Exit east at Oro Dam Blvd for 1.7 mile to Olive Hwy, turn right for 2.1 miles to the casino on the right. RVs should check with Security if they wish to stay overnight.

Rolling Hills Casino
2655 Barham Avenue
Corning, California 96021 — **Map Location #20**
530-528-3500 • 888-331-6400
www.rollinghillscasino.com

Description: The casino has 700 slots, video poker, 14 tables and separate non-smoking areas. Food venues include a deli, buffet and steakhouse. There is a lodge on site.

Discounts: Shasta Club members get senior discounts on Wednesdays and Thursdays.

Directions & Parking: Located 115 miles north of Sacramento, exit I-5 in Corning at Liberal Avenue. The casino is visible from the southbound lanes of the interstate. RVs should park at the front of the lot. Overnight is OK.

Win-River Casino
2100 Redding Rancheria Road
Redding, California 96001 — **Map Location #21**
530-243-3377 • 800-280-8946
www.win-river.com

Description: Located 163 miles north of Sacramento, the casino has 950 slots, 18 gaming tables, craps, an eight-table poker room, bingo, a full service restaurant, snack bar and a comedy club. There is a 96-room Hilton Garden Inn on site.

Directions & Parking: From I-5 exit 667 (Bonnyview), go west on Bonnyview to Hwy-273 south for three stop lights. The casino is about three miles from the interstate. Ample parking is within walking distance to the casino. Please notify Security if you plan to stay overnight.

Cher-Ae Heights Casino
27 Scenic Dr
Trinidad, California 95570 — **Map Location #22**
707-677-3611 • 800-684-2464
www.cheraeheightscasino.com

Description: A friendly casino in a quaint little coastal town features 450 slots in all denominations, 12 pit/gaming tables, separate three-table poker room and bingo five days a week. The casino is open 24 hours daily. The pretty Sunset Restaurant overlooks the ocean with spectacular views from the dining room. It is open from 5pm every evening for dinner and from 10am–1pm for Sunday Brunch. Reservations are suggested. The Sunrise Deli in the casino is open until midnight.

Directions & Parking: From US-101 Trinidad exit (Trinidad Beach sign at exit) immediately turn south on to Scenic Drive for one mile. *Note*:

there are steep grades going up to the casino. Free overnight parking is available for RVs and 24-hour shuttle service is provided.

Blue Lake Casino
777 Casino Way
Blue Lake, California 95525 — **Map Location #22**
707-668-9770
www.bluelakecasino.com

Description: Located ten miles north of Eureka, the casino features 700 slots, 16 gaming tables, the Trillium poker room, Alice's all-you-can-eat Buffet and the 24-hour Lily Pad Café. Free live shows are featured in the Steelhead Lounge with an open dance floor.

Discounts: Nifty Fifty Tuesday offers weekly discounts for seniors. Ask about free gifts for joining the slot club. Red-Eye breakfast buffet in the café, midnight–10am.

Directions & Parking: From US-101 at Arcata, take Hwy-299 east for about five miles to the Blue Lake exit. After entering the casino lot, park in the large open area to the left. Free overnight parking is available.

Elk Valley Casino
2500 Howland Hill Road
Crescent City, California 95531 — **Map Location #23**
707-464-1020 • 888-574-2744
www.elkvalleycasino.com

Description: On the northwest California coast 84 miles north of Eureka, the 23,000 square foot 24/7 casino has several hundred slots, live blackjack and poker at the gaming tables and a 24-hour café.

Discounts: Senior discount at Tuesday lunch.

Directions & Parking: From US-101 south end of Crescent City, go east for 1.1 mile on Elk Valley Road (traffic light at the corner of 101 and Elk

Valley Rd), then south on Howland Hill Road for .6 mile to the casino. Free RV parking is available. Check with Security if you plan to stay overnight; the casino is accommodating for RV guests.

Lucky 7 Casino
350 North Indian Road
Smith River, California 95567 — **Map Location #23**
707-487-7777 • 866-777-7170
www.lucky7casino.com

Description: This 24,000 square foot 24-hour casino is located in the northwestern corner of the state, just three miles south of the Oregon border. It has 300 slots, two blackjack tables and a full service restaurant.

Directions & Parking: The casino is visible from the northbound lanes of the 101 Freeway. Designated RV parking is within walking distance to the casino, and overnight parking is permitted.

Colorado

Casinos in Colorado are located in two historic mining regions of the Rockies: Black Hawk/Central City (off I-70) and Cripple Creek (west of I-25). Two Indian casinos are located in the southern region of the state off U.S. Highway 160.

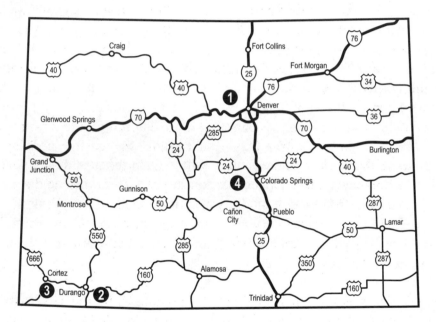

Casino Hopping In The Rockies, page 57

Map	Casino
1	Black Hawk & Central City - 22 casinos
4	Cripple Creek – 15 casinos

Indian Casinos - Southern Colorado, page 60

Map	Casino
2	Sky Ute Casino and Lodge
3	Ute Mountain Casino & RV Park

Casino Hopping in the Rockies

Black Hawk and *Central City* are among Colorado's oldest settlements. These towns grew as a result of the gold rush of 1859 and prospered during the latter half of the 19th Century. After the gold ran out, the area turned to coal (hard rock mining), which provided steady employment through the early part of the 20th Century. After that, the area declined somewhat. In 1990 the old mining towns had a major revival when a successful Colorado ballot initiative allowed limited stakes gambling in the commercial districts of the towns with the proceeds earmarked for historic preservation efforts statewide. Gaming began in Black Hawk/ Central City in 1991, ushering in a new "gold rush" for the historic mining towns.

With some two dozen casinos clustered in the charming little downtown areas, Black Hawk/Central City is a natural for "casino hopping." All casinos have slots, video poker, video blackjack and video keno. Some casinos have table games: blackjack, poker, let it ride and three-card poker. In Colorado a single wager is limited to $5. Casinos in Black Hawk and Central City are open every day 8am–2am. You can find more information about the city of Black Hawk at their web site: www.cityofblackhawk.org.

Cripple Creek is the other area that was revitalized by the 1990 ballot initiative in Colorado. A unique Old West town, Cripple Creek is located in the mountains west of Colorado Springs. It is another interesting historic preservation/casino-hopping location. The Cripple Creek District Museum in the heart of the old mining town reflects the rich history of the area. There are also guided mine tours and gold panning adventures in season. The history of the Old West is also preserved at the theater in Cripple Creek. Some 15 casinos, located on the main thoroughfare in Cripple Creek, all offer electronic gaming and live action gaming tables. Information about Cripple Creek is available from their tourist office at 877-858-GOLD.

Black Hawk & Central City — Map Location #1

Directions: From I-70 exit 244, east on Hwy-6 for 2.8 miles, north on Hwy-119 for 6.7 miles into Black Hawk. Turn left at the first traffic light (Mill Street). Take Mill Street through the intersection of Main Street and continue up the hill for 1.8 miles to the large Miners Mesa Parking area. *Note*: Roads leading to Black Hawk and the parking lot are narrow and winding. Also, Hwy-6 (between I-70 and Hwy-119) has two tunnels with 13 ft. clearances.

Parking: The Miners Mesa Parking lot is located at the highest point in Black Hawk with a bird's eye view of the old mining town below. From the lot you can enjoy a spectacular 360° view of the mountains and even see the Continental Divide. Free overnight parking is provided for boondockers. Free shuttle buses operate daily between 8am and 2am between the Miners Mesa lot and all the casinos in Black Hawk and Central City.

Black Hawk casinos include:

Main Street

> Bull Durham Saloon & Casino, Canyon Casino, Colorado Central Station, Fitzgerald's, Gilpen Hotel Casino, Golden Gates, Isle of Capri, The Lodge, Mardi Gras, Riviera Casino and Wild Card Saloon

Gregory Street

> Black Hawk Station, Bullwackers, Eureka! and Red Dolly

Richman Street

> Ameristar Black Hawk and Richman Casino

Chase Street

> Silver Hawk

Central City casinos include:

Main Street

> Famous Bonanza and Doc Holliday Casino

Gregory Street

> Harvey's Hotel & Casino

Dostal Alley

> Dostal Alley Saloon

Cripple Creek — Map Location #4

Directions: From I-25 exit 141 go west on US-24 to Divide, CO. Then south on Hwy-67 for 18 miles (two-lane road with sharp curves and steep grades) to Cripple Creek.

Parking: There are no designated parking places for RVs at the Cripple Creek casinos and space for RV parking anywhere in town is very limited. There is free daytime parking available on the east side of Hwy-67 coming into town (spaces limited). For overnight, the mountainous terrain prevents camping on casino properties but there is one campground nearby, south of the casinos on Warren Ave, between 2nd and 3rd.

Cripple Creek casinos include:

East Bennett Avenue

> Black Diamond Casino, Brass Ass Casino, Bronco Billy's, Colorado Grande Gaming Parlor, Creeker's Casino, Double Eagle Hotel & Casino, Gold Rush Hotel & Casino, Johnny Nolan's, J.P. McGill's Hotel & Casino, Midnight Rose Hotel & Casino, Uncle Sam's, Virginia Mule and Womack's Legends.

Third Street

> Imperial Hotel & Casino

Myers Avenue

> Wild Horse Casino

General information about Cripple Creek casinos:

- Free shuttle service runs daily.
- Many casinos hand out Fun Books and coupons at the door.
- Some casinos offer free hot dogs, popcorn and drinks for players.
- Ask about daily specials and senior discounts at casino restaurants.

Indian Casinos — Southern Colorado

Sky Ute Casino and Lodge
14826 Highway 172 North
Ignacio, Colorado 81137 — **Map Location #2**
970-563-3000 • 888-842-4180
www.skyutecasino.com

Description: Open 24 hours daily, the casino features 450 slots and table games. The Southern Ute Cultural Center and museum is located next to the casino.

Discounts: 10% restaurant discount if 50 and older.

Directions & Parking: From Jct. US-160 & US-550 (east edge of Durango), east two miles on US-160 to SR-172, then south on SR-172 for 18 miles. Large vehicles may park in the south lot. If staying overnight, please notify Security.

Ute Mountain Casino & RV Park
3 Weeminuche Drive
Towaoc, Colorado 81334 — **Map Location #3**
970-565-8800 • 800-258-8007
970-565-6544 (RV park)
www.utemountaincasino.com

Description: The RV park has 84 level gravel sites (some full hookup, some water & electric), with patio, table and grill. Also, a central dump, laundry facility and swimming pool (in season). Last year's daily rate was $15 and shuttle service is provided to the casino. Ute Tribal Park tours are available. The casino is the largest in the four corners area with over 500 slots and blackjack and poker tables. Hours are 8am–4am.

Discounts: 15% food discount for seniors 55 and older.

Directions: From Jct. US-160 and US-666 in Cortez, south for 10.5 miles.

Connecticut

Connecticut is home to two spectacular casinos: Foxwoods and Mohegan Sun. Although neither has a campground, both have large parking areas for RVs and offer 24-hour shuttle service to the casinos.

The two Connecticut casinos are located just across the Thames River from one another. Directions for "casino hopping" the ten miles from one to the other are also included below.

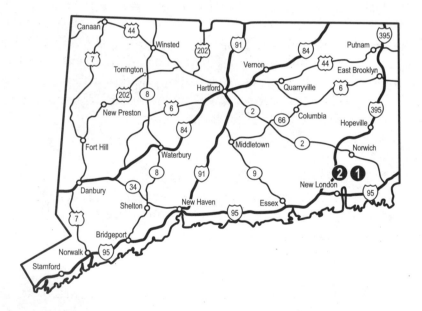

Southeastern Connecticut, page 63

Map	Casino
1	Foxwoods Resort Casino
2	Mohegan Sun Casino

Southeastern Connecticut

Foxwoods Resort Casino
39 Norwich Westerly Road
Mashantucket, CT 06338 — **Map Location #1**
860-312-3000 • 1-800-FOXWOODS
www.foxwoods.com

Description: The famed Foxwoods, with over 300,000 square feet of gaming space, is the largest casino in the world. The Mashantucket Pequot Tribe opened the extraordinary and impressive teal-roofed casino resort in 1992. There are three hotels on property. Foxwoods is so big you'll want to pick up a map at the information booth before exploring the property. Foxwoods has six casinos featuring 6,400 slots, 360 table games, a poker room and ultimate race book. The resort also has 24 restaurants, a Hard Rock Café, two 18-hole championship golf courses and many interesting specialty shops including the Wampum Trading Post Super Store and the Pequot Trader Outlet.

Directions:
From I-95, exit 92, Route 2 west for eight miles to Foxwoods.
From I-84, exit 55, Route 2 east to nine miles past Norwich.
From I-395, exit 85 (in CT), go straight to the second traffic light, then south on Route 164. Follow Route 164 to the end (about seven miles) to Route 2 east for 1.5 miles.

Parking: One of the parking lots on property is designated for large vehicles. Check with Security when you come in. Free overnight parking is permitted. Shuttle service to the casino operates 24 hours.

To get to Mohegan Sun from Foxwoods (approximately ten miles): Exit Foxwoods, turn left on to Route 2 West. Go about four miles to Route 2A. Rosie's Diner will be on your left. Turn left onto 2A. Go to the next stoplight and turn right. Follow Route 2 to next stoplight, which will be Route 12; then turn left. Go approximately 300 yards. Turn right on to Mohegan-Pequot bridge. Once across the bridge, follow signs to Mohegan Sun, which is the first exit on the right.

Mohegan Sun Casino
1 Mohegan Sun Boulevard
Uncasville, CT 06382 — **Map Location #2**
860-862-8000 • 1-888-226-7711
www.mohegansun.com

Description: Mohegan Sun Casino is also large and luxurious. It features a large hotel with more than 1,100 rooms/suites, two casinos with 295,000 square feet of gaming including slots, table games, poker room and a pari-mutuel simulcast facility. It also has a large shopping mall and a wide variety of restaurants plus a food court with specialty food outlets. There is free entertainment nightly in the Wolf Den Showroom.

Directions: From I-95 exit 76, north on I-395 to exit 79A (Route 2A east). It is less than one mile to Mohegan Sun Blvd.

Parking: The "winter" parking lot is designated for large vehicles. Free overnight parking is permitted and 24-hour shuttle service is provided.

To get to Foxwoods from Mohegan Sun (approximately ten miles): Follow Mohegan Sun Blvd to Route 2A East. After crossing Mohegan-Pequot bridge, at the light, turn left onto Route 12. Make the next right on to Route 2A East. Follow it to the end. At the light turn right on to Route 2 East. Follow for four miles to Foxwoods on the right.

Delaware

There are three pari-mutuel facilities with slot machines in the state of Delaware. Only two of them allow overnight RV parking.

Delaware's gaming machines are referred to as VLTs (video lottery terminals) because they are operated by the state's lottery. The machines include traditional slots, video poker, video keno and video blackjack. The minimum gambling age in Delaware is 21 for slots and 18 for horse racing.

Pari-Mutuels With Slots, page 65

Map	Casino
1	Dover Downs Slots
2	Midway Slots & Simulcast

Pari-Mutuels With Slots

Dover Downs Slots
1131 North DuPont Highway
Dover, Delaware 19901 — **Map Location #1**
302-674-4600 • 800-711-5882
www.doverdowns.com

Description: The 91,000 square-foot casino has 2,500 slots, video poker and daily racing simulcasting. There is a 232-room/suite hotel and conference center and nine restaurants from gourmet meals to snacks. Live harness racing takes place November through April. Casino hours are 8am–2am (Mon–Sat) / 1pm–2am (Sun). Dover International Speedway (NASCAR) is located at Dover Downs.

Directions & Parking: Dover Downs is located in the central part of Delaware within the city limits of Dover on the northbound side of US-13, the major north/south highway in Delaware. Motor home parking is on the gravel or grassy portion of the lot at the casino. Overnight parking is permitted.

Midway Slots & Simulcast
Delaware State Fairgrounds
US-13 South
Harrington, Delaware 19952 — **Map Location #2**
302-398-4920 • 888-88-SLOTS
www.midwayslots.com

Description: The casino features 1,437 slots from pennies up and daily simulcasting of horse racing. Live racing takes place at Harrington Raceway April through June, August through October and the Governor's Day Race during the Delaware State Fair in July. Casino hours are 8am–2am/4am (Fri–Sat); noon–2am (Sun). Food venues include the Do-Wop Deli and International Buffet. The casino is open 363 days (closed on Easter and Christmas).

Discounts: Senior discounts are given to those 50 and older.

Directions & Parking: Located 20 miles south of Dover at the State Fairgrounds on US-13. RV parking is available at the far end of the lot along the fence where buses park. Overnight parking is permitted; please check in with Security.

Florida

Florida's Indian tribes operate five 24-hour gaming locations, despite the fact that there is no state/tribal compact in effect. However, the Tampa Hard Rock casino *does not permit* RV parking. RVers are advised to avoid the Tampa casino as they will not allow you to come in.

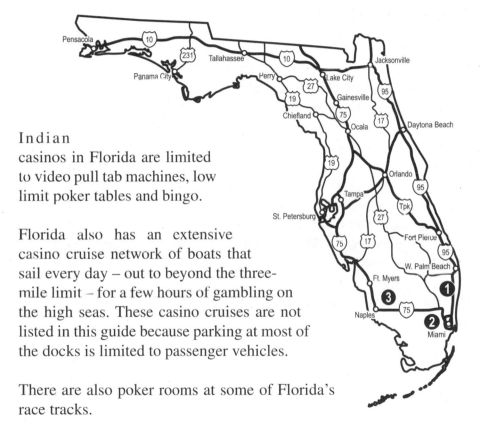

Indian casinos in Florida are limited to video pull tab machines, low limit poker tables and bingo.

Florida also has an extensive casino cruise network of boats that sail every day – out to beyond the three-mile limit – for a few hours of gambling on the high seas. These casino cruises are not listed in this guide because parking at most of the docks is limited to passenger vehicles.

There are also poker rooms at some of Florida's race tracks.

Land-Based Indian Casinos, page 68

Land-Based Indian Casinos

Coconut Creek Casino
5550 NW 40th Street
Coconut Creek, Florida 33073 — **Map Location #1**
954-977-6700 • 866-2-CASINO
www.seminoletribe.com

Description: The 30,000 square-foot casino is located on five acres of Seminole tribal land in the city of Coconut Creek. It has 800 gaming machines, a snack bar and a poker room on the second floor. The casino is open 24 hours every day.

Directions & Parking: Coconut Creek is south of Boca Raton and north of Fort Lauderdale. From I-95 exit 39 go west on Sample Rd for 4.5 miles to NW 54th Ave, turn right and go one-half mile to the casino on the left. (The casino is one block east of US-441). RVs should check with Security for assistance with parking. Although there is a limited parking area, RVs are always welcome; overnight is OK, space permitting.

Hollywood Seminole Gaming
4150 North State Road 7
Hollywood, Florida 33021 — **Map Location #1**
954-961-3220 • 800-323-5452
www.seminoletribe.com

Description: On the Seminole Reservation in Hollywood, Florida, the 130,000 square foot casino has 2,100 gaming machines and 65 poker tables. The resort includes a large hotel, eight nightclubs, 15 restaurants, entertainment venue, shopping mall and a Hard Rock Café.

Directions & Parking: From I-95 exit 22, take Sterling Rd west for three miles to SR-7/US-441. Go south on SR-7 to the casino. Parking for RVs is at the south end of the lot. Check with Security if you plan to be in the lot overnight.

Miccosukee Indian Gaming
500 SW 177th Ave
Miami, Florida 33194 — **Map Location #2**
305-925-2555 • 877-242-6464
www.miccosukee.com

Description: The casino features 1,000 slot and video poker machines that are electronic versions of paper pull tabs, a separate poker room and continuous live bingo. A hotel, conference center, restaurant and snack bar are on site.

Directions & Parking: From the Florida Turnpike Homestead Extension exit 25, go west on US-41 for 5.7 miles, turn right, then left into the parking lot. The casino is located on SR-997 just south of US-41 (a major east-west route across south Florida). It is 11 miles north of Homestead. RVs should park in the Racoon Lot – northwest section of the parking lot, walking distance to the casino. Overnight parking is OK.

Seminole Gaming Palace and Casino
506 South 1st Street
Immokalee, Florida 33934 — **Map Location #3**
239-658-1313 • 800-218-0007
www.seminoletribe.com

Description: The casino, open 24/7, features 550 gaming machines of all denominations and 15 live poker tables with $1 minimums. Food venues include a full service restaurant, bar and snack bar.

Directions & Parking: From I-75 exit 111, east on Hwy-846 (Immokalee Rd) for 35 miles to the casino. There is ample space for RVs to park in the lot. Overnight is OK.

Idaho

Four Indian casinos in Idaho offer electronic gaming. There are no live pit/table games in the state. Two of the casinos have hotels. All four allow free overnight parking for RVs, with free electric hookups available at Coeur D'Alene and a campground at Clearwater. All casinos are open 24/7.

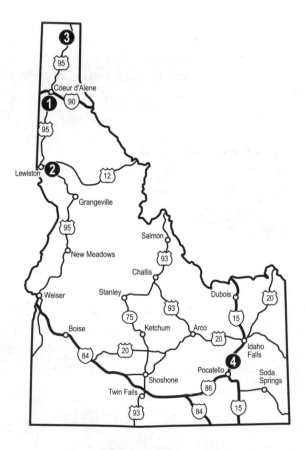

Northwestern Idaho, page 71

Southeastern Idaho, page 73

Northwestern Idaho

Coeur D'Alene Casino Resort Hotel
27068 South Highway 95
Worley, Idaho 83876 — **Map Location #1**
208-686-0248 • 800-523-2464
www.cdacasino.com

Description: The largest casino resort in Idaho has a four star 200-room hotel and conference center designed in dramatic western lodge style. The casino has 1,800 Vegas-style slots (lots of penny machines), video poker and five electronic blackjack tables with seven positions per table and a $5 minimum bet. There is a non-smoking slots area and an OTB room. Food venues include the High Mountain Buffet, the Sweet Grass Café for casual dining overlooking the casino floor and a food court for quick snacks. The buffet restaurant features a deluxe breakfast on Saturdays and Sunday brunch. The 18-hole Circling Raven golf course also has a 25-acre practice facility

Directions & Parking: From I-90 exit 12, south on US-95 for 25 miles (some steep grades, but US-95 is three or four lanes for most of the way). The casino is located directly on US-95 in Worley. RVs should use the parking lot entrance closest to the Chevron station. Free electric hookups are available in the parking lot. If you need assistance with the electric, contact any member of the casino staff.

Clearwater River Casino, Aht'Wy Plaza & Campground
17500 Nez Perce Road
Lewiston, Idaho 83501— **Map Location #2**
208-746-5733 • 877-678-7423
208-750-0231 (RV park)
www.crcasino.com

Description: The small Indian casino has 400 pull tab slots and bingo five days a week. The Riverside Café with about ten tables is inside the casino. Also on the casino property is a gas station and convenience store. There is no hotel at this location. The 33-space full hookup Aht'Wy Campground, adjacent to the casino, is open all year. Most sites are back-in and tight. Dirt roads in the campground tend to be dusty. Last year's rate was $23.

Discounts: A birthday club celebration is held on the last day of the month.

Directions: From I-90 exit 12, south on US-95 for 188 miles. The casino is located on US-95/12 about four miles south of Lewiston. Free overnight RV parking is permitted on the east side of the casino building.

Kootenai River Inn & Casino
7169 Plaza Street (Kootenai River Plaza)
Bonners Ferry, Idaho 83805 — **Map Location #3**
208-267-8511 • 800-346-5668
www.kootenairiverinn.com

Description: The casino resort has a newly-renovated Best Western that has 65 rooms with balconies overlooking the river. It has an indoor pool, fitness center and guest laundry facility. The 30,000 square foot casino features over 400 electronic machines in denominations from pennies up. The Springs Restaurant has menu service daily.

Directions & Parking: The casino resort is located 35 miles south of the Canada border. From I-90 exit 12, travel north on US-95 to Bonners Ferry. The casino is on Hwy-95. Free overnight parking for RVs is available at the far end of the parking lot.

Southeastern Idaho

Fort Hall Casino
Simplot Road (I-15 at exit 80)
Fort Hall, Idaho 83203 — **Map Location #4**
208-237-8778 • 800-497-4231
www.sho-ban.com/gaming.asp

Description: The casino features over 700 slots and has a snack bar. It is open 24/7.

Directions & Parking: From I-15 the casino is visible from the interstate at exit 80. RVs should park toward the back of the lot. Overnight parking is OK.

Illinois

All Illinois casinos are riverboat style. Two casinos have RV parks:

- Empress Casino in Joliet offers a good home base when visiting the Chicago area,
- Casino Queen in East St. Louis is a convenient base for taking in the attractions of the St. Louis area.

Note that some casinos in the state charge admission because of regulations and taxes imposed by the state. Also, some casinos in the Chicago area (including Harrah's in Joliet and Hollywood in Aurora) are in areas too congested to allow for RV parking.

RV-friendly Illinois riverboats include:

- Chicago area: Grand Victoria near I-90 in Elgin,
- Central Illinois: Par-A-Dice next to I-74 in East Peoria and Jumer's Rock Island in the Quad Cities area,
- Downstate: Harrah's Metropolis, off I-24 near the Kentucky state line.

Chicago Area, page 75

East St. Louis Area, page 76

Central & Downstate Illinois, page 77

Chicago Area

Argosy's Empress Casino Hotel & RV Park
2300 Empress Drive
Joliet, Illinois 60436 — **Map Location #1**
815-744-9400 • 888-4-EMPRESS
www.pngaming.com

Description: The RV park has 80 paved sites with patios and electric and water. There is a central dump. A water park is within walking distance. Last year's daily rate was $35. There is also a hotel with an indoor pool in the resort. Shuttle service is provided to the modern casino, The Empress Barge, docked on the Des Plains River that offers a full gaming experience with over 1,100 slots, a variety of table games, a four-table poker room and three restaurants. Casino hours are 8:30am–6:30am daily.

Directions & Parking: <u>Coming from East</u>: take I-80 exit 130, then south on IL Rt-7 (Larkin Ave) for one mile to Rt-6, then west on Rt-6 for 1.5 miles to the casino. <u>Coming from West</u>: take I-80 exit 127, then south on Empress Rd for .6 mile to the end, turn left and go east on Rt-6 for .5 mile to the casino. If staying for a few hours, obtain a permit from Security to park in the lot. If staying overnight, please check in to the RV park. Overnight parking is not allowed in the casino lot.

Grand Victoria Casino
250 South Grove Avenue
Elgin, Illinois 60120 — **Map Location #2**
847-888-1000 • 888-508-1900
www.grandvictoria-elgin.com

Description: The dockside casino on the Fox River has 29,000 square feet of gaming with more than 1,000 slots, 41 pit/gaming tables and three restaurants. The casino is open daily 8:30am–6:30am. Admission is free.

Discounts: Seniors (65 and older) get 10% off the buffet.

Directions & Parking: From I-90 tollway (milepost 24), take Rt-31 south for 2.3 miles to Chicago Ave. Left on Chicago Ave for .3 mile to South Grove Ave, then right for .25 mile. RV parking is available in the north lot. Please check with Security.

East St. Louis Area

Casino Queen
200 South Front Street
East St. Louis, Illinois 62201 — **Map Location #3**
618-874-5000 • 800-777-0777
618-874-5000 – Ext. 8871 (RV park)
www.casinoqueen.com

Description: The 132-space RV park has all large pull-thru sites with full hookups. Also, laundry facilities, a dump station, recreation room area and playground. Free shuttle service operates to and from the casino. Last year's rates were $23–$33 per night. The casino is a four-deck replica of a 19th century side-wheel riverboat. It has 1,200 gaming stations at slots and tables. The buffet restaurant is open for breakfast, lunch and dinner daily. The Sports Bar has 27 TVs and live entertainment on weekends. The casino riverboat is docked on the Mississippi River directly across from St. Louis. Both the RV park and casino have spectacular views of the Gateway Arch and St. Louis skyline. Casino hours are 9am–7am daily.

Discounts: Discounts honored at the RV park include Good Sam, AAA and FMCA. RV guests receive first-day coupons of $5 matchplay for the RV driver and the navigator, two-for-one breakfast and 35% off a gift shop item. Wednesday is Senior Day at the casino.

Directions: From I-70/I-55 westbound, use exit 2A (3rd St) or eastbound use exit 1/downtown (4th St), then follow casino signs. From I-255, exit 17B follow brown riverboat casino signs. Boondocking is also permitted in the truck parking lot just outside of the RV park entrance.

Central & Downstate Illinois

Par-A-Dice Casino
21 Blackjack Boulevard
East Peoria, Illinois 61611 — **Map Location #4**
309-698-7711 • 800-332-5634
www.par-a-dice.com

Description: The riverboat casino docked on the Illinois River is located just a mile from I-74 with easy on/off from the interstate. The boat has four decks featuring 34 tables and 1,150 slots plus four restaurants. Casino hours are 10am–6am daily.

Directions & Parking: From I-74 exit 95B, one mile north on Main St.

The casino is on the left. Use the lot behind the hotel where designated RV spaces are along the back perimeter of the parking lot. The casino is within walking distance.

Jumer's Casino Rock Island
1735 First Avenue
Rock Island, Illinois 61201 — **Map Location #5**
309-793-4200 • 800-477-7747
www.jumerscri.com

Description: The paddlewheeler riverboat casino is docked on the Mississippi River and is open 8am–3am daily. It has five floors of gaming including slots, video poker, pit/table games, restaurant and café.

Directions & Parking: From I-74 exit 2, take Hwy-92 west to the riverboat. Free parking is available for RVs, but there are low overhang hazards near the RV lot. Please check in with Security if you plan to stay overnight, and use extra caution when exiting the RV lot.

Harrah's Metropolis
203 South Ferry Street
Metropolis, Illinois 62960 — **Map Location #6**
618-524-2628 • 800-935-7700
www.harrahs.com

Description: Harrah's is in southern Illinois across from Paducah, KY where the Ohio River meets I-24. It features 1,200 slots, 25 pit/table games and two restaurants: Fresh Market Square Buffet and The Range Steakhouse. Casino hours are 9am–7am daily. There is a hotel on site.

Directions & Parking: From I-24 exit 37, west on Rt-45 to Ferry Street in Metropolis. Turn left and follow Ferry St to the casino. Use the perimeter of the parking lot where there are designated spots for RVs. Use caution when entering and exiting the parking lot to avoid bottoming out. Overnight parking is permitted for self-contained vehicles.

Indiana

Indiana legalized casinos in 1993. Counties located along either Lake Michigan or the Ohio River are eligible to have riverboat casinos. Today Indiana has ten dockside casinos.

Five riverboats are on Lake Michigan in the greater Chicago metropolitan area. These facilities – two in Gary and one each in Hammond, Michigan City and East Chicago – are not recommended for large RVs. Traffic is generally congested and parking is very tight.

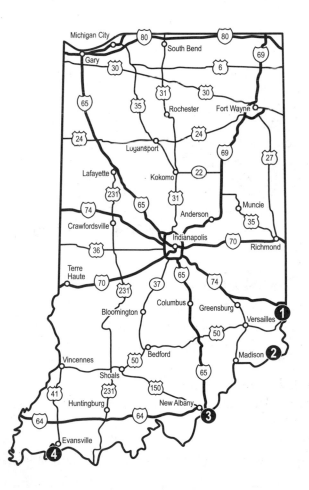

The five casinos on the Ohio River along the State's eastern and southern border, on the other hand, are in less densely populated areas and are accessible from major interstates. They are all RV-friendly, providing designated parking areas for large vehicles. Argosy and Grand Victoria are down river west of Cincinnati, OH. Belterra and Caesars (to be renamed Horseshoe by 2007) are across the Ohio River from the Louisville, KY area and Casino Aztar is docked on the Ohio in the southern most tip of the state.

Indiana's 11th casino, Blue Sky Casino Resort at the site of the former French Lick Springs Resort/Spa in southern Indiana, is scheduled to open in December 2006. It will include a casino, hotel, golf course and event center.

Riverboats On The Ohio River, page 80

Map	Casino
1	Argosy Casino and Hotel
1	Grand Victoria Casino & Resort
2	Belterra Casino and Resort
3	Caesars Indiana
4	Casino Aztar

Riverboats On The Ohio River

Argosy Casino and Hotel
777 Argosy Parkway
Lawrenceburg, Indiana 47025 — **Map Location #1**
812-539-8000 • 888-ARGOSY-7
www.pngaming.com

Description: A 4,000 passenger modern yacht, Argosy is open 24 hours daily. The 74,000 square feet of gaming includes 2,200 slots, table games and four restaurants. Admission is $3/$5. Reservations are suggested on holidays and weekends. A 300-room hotel is connected to the casino.

Discounts: Seniors 55+ get $1 off admission all day Sunday–Thursday and 9am–5pm Friday and Saturday.

Directions & Parking: From I-275 west exit 16, take US-50 west. Follow brown riverboat signs. From I-74 exit 164, south on Rt-1 for approximately 14 miles to US-50. Follow brown riverboat signs. The RV parking lot is on US-50 at Lorey Lane (about a mile northwest of the casino). Overnight is OK and daily 24-hour shuttle service is provided.

Grand Victoria Casino & Resort
600 Grand Victoria Drive
Rising Sun, Indiana 47040 — **Map Location #1**
812-438-1234 • 800-GRAND-11
www.hyatt.com

Description: This pretty paddle wheeler has 29 tables and 1,500 slots on four levels; top level is non-smoking. Roulette is single zero. Casino hours are 8am–5am/24hrs (Fri–Sat). The resort has a hotel and Southern Indiana's only Scottish-links style golf course. There are four restaurants and a sports bar at the casino.

Discounts: 10% for seniors, 55+ seasonally. Ask about the current senior discounts.

Directions & Parking: From the Cincinnati area, I-275 west to exit 16, west on US-50 for 6.9 miles, then south on Rt-56 for 7.8 miles. This takes you through the historic town of Aurora and on a scenic byway along the picturesque Ohio River. Turn left at Grand Victoria Drive. RVs should park in the large lot on the right – sections 6 and 7. The parking lot is walking distance to the casino. Overnight parking is permitted for self-contained RVs.

Belterra Casino and Resort
777 Belterra Drive
Belterra, Indiana 47020 — **Map Location #2**

812-427-4008 • 888-BELTERRA
www.belterracasino.com

Description: The 38,000 square foot casino includes 41 gaming tables
and 1,500 slots in all denominations. Hours of operation are 8am–4am/
5am (Fri–Sat). The resort has a hotel, five restaurants and a Tom Fazio-
designed 7,000-yard golf course.

Directions & Parking: From I-71 in Kentucky, exit 57 (Warsaw/Sparta),
west on Rt-35 toward Warsaw, KY. At Rt-42 turn left toward the
Markland Dam bridge and turn left on to the bridge. After crossing the
bridge, turn left at the stop sign to the casino. RVs should park in the
large open area parking lot; overnight is OK.

Caesars Indiana (to be renamed Horseshoe by 2007)
11999 Avenue of the Emperors
Elizabeth, Indiana 47117 — **Map Location #3**
812-969-6000 • 888-ROMAN-4-U
www.caesarsindiana.com

Description: The 5,000-passenger "Glory of Rome" is billed as the
world's largest riverboat. Open 24 hours daily, the casino has over 100
pit/gaming tables, 2,800 slots and a buffet restaurant. There is a 500-
room hotel at the resort.

Discounts: Wednesday is Senior Day (55+) at Caesars/Horseshoe. Ask
about the current discounts.

Directions & Parking: From I-64 exit 123 (New Albany), go straight for
two blocks to Main St. Turn right on Main St to Hwy-111 south (road
bears to left). Take Hwy-111 south for eight miles to Caesars/Horseshoe
on the right. RVs should drive past the parking garage and turn right on
Stucky Rd to the outdoor lot designated for large vehicles. Overnight
RV parking is permitted.

Casino Aztar
421 N.W. Riverside Drive
Evansville, Indiana 47708 — **Map Location #4**
812-433-4000 • 800-DIAL-FUN
www.casinoaztar.com

Description: Aztar is an old fashioned paddle wheeler featuring 361 gaming positions at 47 tables and 1,350 slots including the newest video slots. Prior to entering the boat, stop at the rewards booth and get a Premium Passenger Club Card, which will give you free admission to the casino. For those who don't have a card, admission is $3. Casino hours are 8am–5am/24 hrs (Fri–Sun). The hotel at the resort has 250 rooms and four restaurants and live entertainment is featured on weekends.

Discounts: Monday is Senior Day at Aztar; free coffee and donuts and 25% off all restaurants and the gift shop if 55 and older. Seniors get 10% off food on all other days.

Directions & Parking: From I-64 exit 25, south on Rt-41 for approximately 15 miles to the Lloyd Expressway, then west to Fulton Ave and south for three blocks. Free overnight parking is available in the lot.

Iowa

Iowa's gaming includes riverboats, Indian casinos and pari-mutuels. In eastern Iowa, six riverboats are docked along the Mississippi River and a pari-mutuel greyhound park/casino is located in Dubuque. Central Iowa is home to two casino resorts and a pari-mutuel/casino gaming complex. Western Iowa has three riverboats on the Missouri River, two Indian-owned casinos and a pari-mutuel greyhound park and casino.

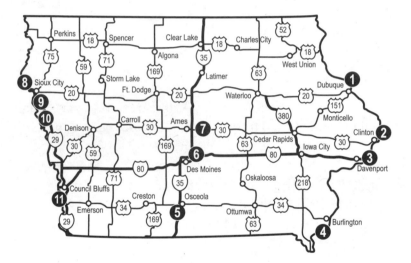

In 2004 Iowa passed legislation permitting gaming tables to be added to the casinos at its three pari-mutuels located in Dubuque, Altoona and Council Bluffs.

In 2005, four new casinos received gaming licenses:

- **Diamond Jo Worth Casino** in Northwood is scheduled to open in early 2006. It will be located directly next to the Top Of Iowa Welcome Center on I-35 exit 214. The casino will permit RV parking and there is a dump station at the welcome center.

- **Wild Rose Casino & RV Park** on US-18 one mile east of Emmetsburg is slated to open in July 2006. The resort complex will be on 90 acres and will include a state-of-the-art casino, 54-room hotel and a 100-site RV park. More information about the new casino is available at www.wildroseresorts.com.

- **Isle of Capri** will build a riverboat casino in Waterloo at the Lost Island Water Park. It will include a hotel and camping facilities and may be opened in 2006.

- **Washington County Casino & Golf Resort**, a glitzy resort on 325 acres, will include a casino, hotel, RV park and golf course and is expected to open in late 2007.

Eastern Iowa, page 86

Map	Casino
1	Dubuque Diamond Jo Casino
1	Dubuque Greyhound Park & Casino
2	Mississippi Belle II
3	Isle of Capri – Bettendorf
4	Catfish Bend Casino

Central Iowa, page 89

Map	Casino
5	Terrible's Lakeside Casino Resort and RV Park
6	Prairie Meadows Racetrack & Casino
7	Meskwaki Bingo & Casino & RV Sites

Western Iowa, page 91

Map	Casino
8	Argosy's Belle of Sioux City Casino
9	Winnavegas
10	Casino Omaha
11	Bluffs Run Raceway / Horseshoe Casino
11	Harrah's Council Bluffs Casino
11	Ameristar Casino Council Bluffs

Eastern Iowa

Dubuque Diamond Jo Casino
Third Street Ice Harbor
Dubuque, Iowa 52004 — **Map Location #1**
563-583-7005 • 800-LUCKY-JO
www.diamondjo.com

Description: The old-fashioned steamboat replica is open daily 7am–3am/24 hrs on weekends. The riverboat casino has 750 slots, 16 pit/gaming tables and a poker room. There are two dockside restaurants. Outdoor concerts are held seasonally at Grandstand Under The Stars. The Grand Harbor Resort is next door to the casino. It has 193 rooms overlooking the river, a large arcade and indoor water park. There is a picturesque walking path behind the hotel along the banks of the mighty Mississippi.

Discounts: Players Club members get 20% off the buffet if 55+ and 25% discount in the gift shop every day.

Directions & Parking: From Rt-20 Locust Street exit in downtown Dubuque, north on Locust to Third St, east on Third for three blocks to the casino. Cross the bridge to the casino and go to the lot on the left. RV spaces with free electric hookups are located along the white fence.

Dubuque Greyhound Park & Casino
1855 Greyhound Park Drive
Dubuque, Iowa 52001 — **Map Location #1**
563-582-3647 • 800-373-3647
www.dgpc.com

Description: This gaming facility has 1,000 slots, gaming tables, live greyhound racing May through October, and simulcast dog and horse racing. There are two delis and a restaurant on site. Hours are 8am–3am/24 hrs on weekends.

Directions & Parking: The Greyhound Park & Casino is located off Hwy-151/61 at the Dubuque-Wisconsin Bridge. From Rt-20 exit at Downtown Dubuque to Hwy-151/61 North. Parking for oversize vehicles is behind the casino building. Overnight RV parking is permitted.

Mississippi Belle II
311 Riverview Drive
Clinton, Iowa 52732 — **Map Location #2**
563-243-9000 • 800-457-9973

Description: The Mississippi Belle II is open 9am–4am. Aboard the Belle are 500 slots and 14 pit/gaming tables. Food venues include the Captain's Deli for lunch and dinner and the 40-Feet-of-Fine-Food Buffet morning to night. Live entertainment on weekends.

Directions & Parking: From I-80 exit 306, take US-67 north to US-30, then US-30 east (Camanche Ave) through the business district. It becomes a one-way street (3rd) at the Hyvee Market. Stay on that road for about a mile to 6th Ave N. Turn right on 6th Ave, go through the light and over the tracks to the large parking lot on the left. Free overnight parking is permitted for RVs in the lot; shuttle service to the casino is provided. There are also some RV spaces with hookups in a city parking area adjacent to the casino lot.

Isle of Capri – Bettendorf
1821 State Street
Bettendorf, Iowa 52722 — **Map Location #3**
563-359-7280 • 800-724-5825
www.isleofcapricasino.com

Description: The 2,500 passenger paddle wheeler on the Mississippi River is less than a mile from I-74 with easy on/off access. The casino features over 1,000 slots, 35 pit/gaming tables and live action in the poker room. Food venues include: Calypso's Buffet, Tradewinds Marketplace and Farradday's Restaurant. Penguin's Comedy Club has live entertainment. The riverboat is open 24 hours daily. An adjacent hotel has 292 rooms/suites and convention and meeting space. The marina has 70 docking spaces.

Discounts: Ask about senior (age 50+) discounts offered on Tuesdays and Thursdays. These may include 50% off on gift shop items, two-for-one on meals or match play in the casino.

Directions & Parking: From I-74 exit 4 (State St), east on State St for .4 mile. Turn left at 17th St. After you cross the George Theunen Bridge into the casino complex there are two lots that can accommodate RVs. The west lot is designated for trucks and RVs; the large self-park lot on the east side is nearest to the casino. Free overnight RV parking is permitted.

Catfish Bend Casino
902 Riverview Drive
Fort Madison, Iowa 52627 — **Map Location #4**
319-372-2946 • 800-372-2946
www.catfishbendcasino.com

Description: The 1,500-passenger paddlewheeler is docked in Fort Madison during warm weather months. The casino is open 8am–2am (Sun-Mon) and 24 hrs (Tue–Sat). The 14,500 square-foot gaming area has 1,200 slots in all denominations and various table games. A poker room is on the second level. The all-you-can-eat Bourbon Street Buffet on the top deck is open daily for lunch and dinner and a Sunday champagne brunch features live piano music.

Note: From November to April the boat moves up river to Burlington, Iowa.

Discounts: Senior discounts are extended to those 50 and older. Ask about Monday buffet discounts for slot club members.

Directions & Parking: From I-280 in the Quad City area, south on US-61 through Fort Madison. Go through town; the casino is located on the east side of US-61. Free RV parking is available in the bus lot.

Central Iowa

Terrible's Lakeside Casino Resort and RV Park
777 Casino Drive
Osceola, Iowa 50213 — **Map Location #5**
641-342-9511 • 877-477-5253
www.terribleherbst.com

Description: This lakeside resort, located next to I-35 in central Iowa, has a modern RV park and a 60-room (all suites) hotel with outdoor pool and hot tub. The RV park, with 47 full hookup pull-thru sites, is open all year. RV check-in is in the casino lobby; daily rate in 2005 was $15. The casino, an old-fashioned paddle wheeler on West Lake, is open 24 hours and has 1,000 slots, 24 gaming tables and a poker room. The boat remains dockside. The Wheelhouse Buffet features all-you-can-eat dining for breakfast, lunch and dinner and the Landing Steakhouse offers fine dining. A fishing and boating dock is also available at the resort.

Discounts: Monday is senior day at Lakeside; ask about discounts currently being offered for people 50 and older. RV daily rate is discounted to $10 with a Players Club card.

Directions: From I-35 exit 34, west for .2 mile on Clay St to the resort. It is suggested that RVs go into the RV park. However, if you wish to boondock, park in the north area of the lot and do not put your jacks down.

Prairie Meadows Racetrack & Casino
1 Prairie Meadows Drive
Altoona, Iowa 50009 — **Map Location #6**
515-967-1000 • 800-325-9015
www.prairiemeadows.com

Description: Prairie Meadows is the nation's first "racino" (casino gaming and racing at the same location). The 24-hour casino has 1,500 slot machines, video poker, 33 gaming tables, nine-table poker room, buffet restaurant and free entertainment. The track features live horse racing throughout the summer and simulcast racing.

Discounts: Club 55 for senior citizens offers discounts, special promotions and entertainment for seniors 55 and older.

Directions & Parking: Prairie Meadows is located near I-80 exit 142 next to Adventureland. There is a specific parking area for large vehicles, but "no overnight parking" signs are posted. RVs should not put down their jacks in the parking lot.

Meskwaki Bingo & Casino & RV Sites
1504 305th Street
Tama, Iowa 52339 — **Map Location #7**
641-484-2108 • 800-728-4263
www.meskwaki.com

Description: The 24-hour casino features 1,325 slots, 26 pit/table games, live keno, racing simulcast, poker room and a high limits gaming area. Weekly tournaments are held in the poker room. There is a separate non-smoking slots area. Bingo is held seven days a week. Dining choices include the 24-hour River's Edge Buffet, Garden Park Deli and a concession area. There is a 206-room hotel at the resort. Live entertainment is featured in the Garden Park Showroom.

Directions & Parking: From I-80 exit 191/Tama, north on US-63 (two-lane) for 22.8 miles to US-30 (traffic light at junction of US-63/30). Go west on US-30 for 4.4 miles to the casino on the south side of US-30. — or — From I-35 exit 111, go 47 miles east to the casino, (US-30 is a major thoroughfare and opens to four lanes in some areas). The casino is located directly on US-30. RV sites with free electric and water are on the grassy area south of the casino and are available on a first-come, first-serve basis.

Western Iowa

Argosy's Belle of Sioux City Casino
100 Larsen Park Road
Sioux City, Iowa 51101 — **Map Location #8**
712-294-5600 • 800-424-0080
www.pngaming.com

Description: The triple-deck 1920's styled paddle wheel replica on the Missouri River, features an open-air deck from which you can take in the picturesque riverfront. The 24-hour casino has 450 slots, 19 tables and a poker room. There are two restaurants – one is open 24 hours.

Directions & Parking: The casino, at I-29 exit 147, is visible from the southbound lanes of the interstate. The south end parking lot is designated for RVs and overnight parking is OK; 24-hour casino shuttle service is available every 15 minutes.

Winnavegas
1500 330th Street
Sloan, Iowa 51055 — **Map Location #9**
712-428-9466 • 800-468-9466
www.winnavegas-casino.com

Description: Located in a quiet, restful farm area 20 miles south of Sioux City, the neat and clean 24-hour casino is owned and operated by the Winnebago Tribe of Nebraska. The casino features 900 slots, video poker, 26 pit/table games and a separate poker room. The Flowers Island Restaurant is open 7am–10pm and has buffet and menu service.

Directions & Parking: From I-29 exit 127, west on 330th St. The casino is three miles from the interstate. There are 14 electric hookup sites available for $7 per night. RV check-in is at the casino. Free RV parking is permitted in the north parking lot. There is a free dump station and a fresh water supply is available.

Casino Omaha
1 Blackbird Bend
Onawa, Iowa 51040 — **Map Location #10**
712-423-3700 • 800-858-U-BET

Description: Casino Omaha features 550 slots, ten gaming tables and a restaurant. Hours are 8am–3am/24hrs (Fri–Sat). Blackbird Bend Raceway, IMCA sanctioned, is located next to the casino. A gas station is across from the casino.

Discounts: A $1.99 breakfast is served Monday through Saturday. Coupons are available at the slot club booth on some weekdays.

Directions & Parking: From I-29 exit 112, west for .6 mile to the flashing yellow light, north on Dogwood Ave for .8 mile to the stop sign, then west on Hwy-K-42 for 2.3 miles. Turn left at the casino sign, then .9 mile to the casino. Ample parking is available for RVs, but it's noisy until about midnight on race nights.

Bluffs Run Raceway/Horseshoe Casino
2701 23rd Avenue
Council Bluffs, Iowa 51501 — **Map Location #11**
712-323-2500 • 800-BET-2-WIN
www.harrahs.com

Description: Bluffs Run, a premier greyhound park, has live dog racing Tue–Sun in season, as well as horse race simulcasting. The expanded 24-hour casino (renamed Horseshoe Council Bluffs and open in Spring 2006) features 1,900 slots, various table games, poker room and non-smoking section. Restaurants include Grand Buffet, the Winner's Grill and Fireside Steakhouse.

The RV park at Bluffs Run closed in mid-2005 and is not expected to reopen.

Directions & Parking: From I-80/I-29 exit 1B, north .5 mile on 24th St to 23rd Ave, west on 23rd for .4 mile —or— From I-29 exit 52, follow casino signs. The track/casino complex is visible from the westbound lanes of I-80. Free overnight RV parking is permitted in the northeast lot of the casino for up to 12 hours.

Harrah's Council Bluffs Casino
One Harrah's Boulevard
Council Bluffs, Iowa 51501 — **Map Location #11**
712-329-6000 • 800-HARRAHS
www.harrahs.com

Description: On the Missouri River, Harrah's riverboat casino features three decks of gaming with 1,300 slots, 30 pit/gaming tables and a live action poker room. There are three food venues, including a 24-hour diner. There is a 251-room hotel and an 18-hole golf course is adjacent to the casino. The riverboat remains dockside and is open 24 hours every day.

Directions & Parking: Located at I-29 exit 53. RVs should park in the north lot and check with Security if you plan to stay overnight.

Ameristar Casino Council Bluffs
2200 River Road
Council Bluffs, Iowa 51501 — **Map Location #11**
712-328-8888 • 877-IMASTAR
www.ameristarcasinos.com

Description: Ameristar II is Iowa's largest riverboat and features casino action on three levels with 1,500 slot and video poker machines and 30 pit/table games. There is a 160-room dockside hotel. Restaurants include: Waterfront Grill, Veranda Buffet, Amerisports Bar and Prairie Mill Café and Bakery that features traditional country-style regional favorites. The riverboat remains dockside and is open 24/7.

Discounts: Seniors (55+) receive a 15% discount.

Directions & Parking: Ameristar II is located just west of I-29 at exit 52 (Nebraska Ave). Designated parking for large vehicles is in the south lot (follow "truck parking" signs). RVs should be advised the parking lot is very crowded on weekends. Boondocking overnight is OK.

Kansas

Four Indian-owned casinos located in northeastern Kansas are convenient to US Highway 75, a major north/south highway that crosses Interstate 70 at milepost 358. All four casino facilities are RV-friendly. Harrah's has a modern RV park, while Golden Eagle, Sac and Fox, and White Cloud all have RV sites with hookups in their parking areas.

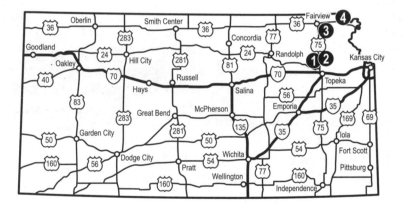

Northeastern Kansas, page 95

Northeastern Kansas

Harrah's Prairie Band Casino & RV Park
12305 150th Road
Mayetta, Kansas 66509 — **Map Location #1**
785-966-7777 • 800-HARRAHS
877-2-RVPARK (RV park reservations)
www.harrahs.com

Description: Located in the Kansas heartland, this Harrah's 24-hour casino is owned by the Prairie Band Potowatomi Nation. The resort has a 300-room hotel and a pleasant RV park. There are 67 paved, full-hookup sites, two bathhouses and laundry facilities in the RV park. Phone hookups are available at each site and wi-fi is being installed. All sites are pull-thrus and have cable TV and picnic tables. Free 24-hour shuttle service is provided to the casino. Last year's RV rates were $15–$25. The casino has 1,100 slots in all denominations, 30 pit/gaming tables, a poker room, buffet restaurant, fine dining steakhouse and the Prairie Pub. An on-site convention center is a venue for concerts and special events.

Discounts: Incentive discounts at the RV park include cash back casino coupons for every night stayed, two-for-one buffet coupons and casino matchplay. On Wednesdays senior citizens get $5 off at the buffet.

Directions & Parking: From I-70 exit 358, north on US-75 for 17 miles, then west on 150th Ave for 1.8 mile to Harrah's. Follow signs to the RV park adjacent to the casino. Boondocking is also permitted at the far end of the casino lot.

Golden Eagle Casino
1121 Goldfinch Road
Horton, Kansas 66489 — **Map Location #2**
785-486-6601 • 888-464 5825
www.goldeneaglecasino.com

Description: Owned and operated by the Kickapoo Tribe, the casino is open 24/7. It has over 800 slots, 12 pit/gaming tables (including 25¢ roulette and $3 minimum blackjack), seven-table poker room, restaurant and 24-hour snack bar. RV spaces with full hookup are located on the west side of the parking lot. Last year's rate was $10; register in the gift shop. Bingo is held Wed–Sun. Live entertainment is featured on weekends.

Discount: Celebrants get a free meal during their birthday and anniversary month. Senior Day is Wednesday.

Directions & Parking: From I-70 exit 358, north on US-75 for 42 miles to SR-20, east for 4.8 miles; follow casino signs. Free RV parking is also allowed, but Security should be notified if you are staying overnight.

Sac and Fox Casino & RV Spaces
1322 US Highway 75
Powhattan, Kansas 66527 — **Map Location #3**
785-467-8000 • 800-990-2946
www.sacandfoxcasino.com

Description: Open 24 hours daily, the casino features 450 slots and 11 pit/gaming tables with $3 minimum blackjack on weekdays. The Lodge Restaurant features buffets on weekends and menu service weekdays. Also, a deli, golf driving range and a 24-hour truck stop. RV spaces with electric hookup are available in the parking lot; last year's rates were $10. Register at the casino. There is also a central dump station and fresh water available for RVs.

Discounts: Seniors, 55 and older, get $1 off meals. Celebrants receive a free meal during their birthday and anniversary months.

Directions & Parking: From I-70 exit 358, the casino is on the northbound side of US-75 about 44 miles north of Topeka. Adequate parking is provided for large vehicles. If not registered for electric hookups, please notify Security if you plan to stay overnight.

Casino White Cloud & RV Spaces
777 Jackpot Drive
White Cloud, Kansas 66094 — **Map Location #4**
785-595-3430 • 877-652-6115

Description: This charming little Indian casino is surrounded by farmland in the northeastern corner of Kansas, near the Missouri and Nebraska borders. The casino has 450 slots and 11 gaming tables with $3 minimum blackjack on weekdays. The Lodge Restaurant and a deli are the food venues. Casino hours are 9am–1am/3am weekends. There are six full-hookup RV sites adjacent to the parking lot; there is no charge for these spaces, but please register with Security before pulling in. There is no hotel at this location.

Directions: From I-70 exit 358 in KS, go north on US-75 for 58 miles, then east on US-36 for 11 miles, then right on to E Miami St for 4.8 miles (narrow two-lane road), then left on Prairie Rd for 9 miles, then left on Thrasher to the casino. A shorter route out of St. Joseph, MO is to take US-36 west for 18 miles, then SR-7 north for 34 miles.

Louisiana

Louisiana has 13 riverboat casinos: three in the New Orleans area, two in Baton Rouge; three in Lake Charles and five in the Shreveport area. The largest single-level riverboat casino in the world, L'Auberge du Lac, is docked in western Louisiana, but RVs are NOT allowed on their property.

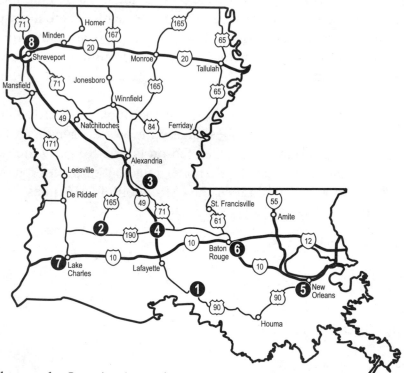

L'Auberge du Lac is the only Louisiana riverboat that prohibits RVs. All others are RV-Friendly. The Isle of Capri in the Shreveport area has a modern RV park and Isle of Capri in Lake Charles has RV spaces with electric hookups. Advance reservations are suggested for both of these Isle locations as the spaces fill up fast.

Three land-based Indian casinos all have RV parks. They are: Cypress Bayou in Charenton, Grand Casino in Kinder and Paragon in Marksville.

All casinos in Louisiana are open 24/7.

Evangeline Downs is a popular "racino" (race track and casino in a single facility) located in Opelousas just off I-49. Other racinos can be found near Lake Charles and in Bossier City.

Riverboat casinos in the Shreveport/Bossier City area offer a good opportunity for "casino-hopping" if you travel with a dinghy or tow vehicle. Each of the five casinos in the area has a distinctive theme – Sam's Town and Eldorado on the west side of the Red River are in walking distance of each other. Boomtown, Horseshoe and Isle of Capri are just across the river and a short drive from one another. The best place to park in Shreveport/Bossier City is at the Isle of Capri RV Park. Check the individual casino listings if you plan to dry camp.

When traveling in Louisiana, you'll also notice a number of smaller "casinos," in travel centers, gas stations and bars. They have limited video gaming machines and no pit/table play.

NOTE RE: 2005 HURRICANE DAMAGE: Despite the hurricanes of 2005, all Louisiana casinos listed in this section are open, except for Bally's Lakeshore Resort (closed indefinitely) and Harrah's in Lake Charles (expected to reopen by 2006).

Land-Based Casinos, page 100

Map	Casino
1	Cypress Bayou Casino & RV Park
2	Coushatta Casino Resort & RV Park
3	Paragon Casino Resort & RV Park
4	Evangeline Downs Racetrack & Casino

Riverboats - New Orleans Area, page 103

Map	Casino
5	Bally's Casino Lakeshore Resort

5   Boomtown Casino - Westbank
5   Treasure Chest Casino

Riverboats - Baton Rouge, page 105

Map   *Casino*
6   Casino Rouge

Riverboats - Lake Charles, page 106

Map   *Casino*
7   Harrah's Lake Charles
7   Isle of Capri Casino & RV Spaces - Lake Charles

Riverboats - Shreveport / Bossier City, page 108

Map   *Casino*
8   Isle of Capri Casino Resort & RV Park - Bossier City
8   Boomtown Casino - Bossier City
8   Horseshoe Casino Hotel - Bossier City
8   Sam's Town Shreveport
8   Eldorado Casino Shreveport

Land-Based Casinos

Cypress Bayou Casino & RV Park
832 Martin Luther King Road
Charenton, LA 70523 — **Map Location #1**
337-923-7284 • 800-284-4386
337-829 5500 (RV park information)
www.cypressbayou.com

Description: The RV park has 11 modern full-hookup paved sites with picnic tables. This is a "self-park" RV park. When you come in, select a site, back in and hook up. 2005 fee was $25 per night or $10 with comment card (see discounts). A casino courtesy shuttle is available.

The 125,000 square foot casino features 1,300 slots and video poker machines and 42 pit/table games. There is a separate non-smoking slots area. The casino is open noon–2am/4am (weekends & holidays). Food venues include Mr. Lester's Steakhouse fine dining, Café Bayou buffet, Eats and Dogs fast food. Cypress Bayou is owned and operated by the Chitimacha Tribe of Louisiana.

Discounts: The fee at the RV park is discounted to $10 if you fill out a comment card and bring it to the Security office for validation.

Directions: From I-10 exit 103A, take US-90 east (along the future I-49 corridor) for 42.5 miles to SR-83, then east on SR-83 and left on SR-182 for .5 mile. Turn right on to Ralph Darden Memorial Pkwy for two miles to the casino. The self-park RV park is east of the casino.

Coushatta Casino Resort & RV Park
777 Coushatta Drive
Kinder, Louisiana 70648 — **Map Location #2**
337-738-1370 • 800-58-GRAND
888-774-7263 (RV park)
www.gccoushatta.com

Description: The RV Resort at Red Shoes Park is set on 40 acres and features 100 paved, full hookup sites and 100 chalets. The park has a two-acre lake with pier, swimming pool complex with two bathhouses, horseshoes, tennis, basketball and volleyball courts, a lodge with fireplace, game room and large screen TV, convenience store, modern laundry facility and large covered deck. Last year's RV rates were $17 on weekdays and $22 weekends. There is a 460 room/suite hotel on site. The casino includes 3,200 slots, 80 gaming tables, a live poker room and high stakes gaming salons. It is open 24 hours daily. The resort also has six restaurants and an 18-hole golf course, Koasati Pines, the longest championship course in the state. Free shuttle service is provided to and from the casino and the golf course. The luxury resort is owned by the Coushatta Tribe of Louisiana. The RV park is named for an 18th century Coushatta leader known as "Red Shoes" who led a small band of tribes people from Alabama to settle the lower reaches of the Red River in Louisiana.

Discounts: Discounts honored at Red Shoes Park are: 10% for Good Sam, FMCA or AARP, 15% for Escapees and $10 per night for Recreation USA. (No multiple discounts.)

Directions & Parking: From I-10 exit 44, north 23 miles on highway 165 (two-lane road) to the resort located five miles north of Kinder. Free parking is available for RVs on the service road just outside the RV park entrance. RVs are not permitted to park in the main parking lot.

Paragon Casino Resort & RV Park
711 Paragon Place
Marksville, Louisiana 71351 — **Map Location #3**
318-253-1946 • 800-WIN-1-WIN
www.paragoncasinoresort.com

Description: The resort includes a large hotel and an RV park. There are 166 paved pull-thru RV sites with full hookups including cable TV. The RV park has a pool, laundry facilities, horseshoes, volleyball and a large guest lodge with a big screen TV. Last year's RV rates were from $13 per night. Five food venues at the casino feature casual and fine dining, a Cajun bistro, a diner and the buffet. The resort includes an 18-hole championship golf course. Free shuttle service is provided to the casino and golf course. The 75,000 square foot, 24-hour casino has over 2,100 slot machines in all denominations with Las Vegas odds, 46 gaming tables, a poker room, Diamond Room for high denomination slot play and Emerald Room for high denomination table play.

Discounts: The RV park honors Good Sam and Passport America discounts. Group discounts are also given and the large covered patio and clubhouse are available for group use. At the casino, ladies receive a free dinner buffet on the third Thursday and men receive a free dinner buffet on the second Tuesday. Players Club card and ID must be shown for free buffets. Seasonal promotions may include valuable gifts or match play for new Players Club members. Ask about current promotions at the Players Club desk.

Directions: From I-49 exit 46 in Alexandria, take LA-1 south for 32 miles to the casino complex on the right.

Evangeline Downs Racetrack & Casino
2435 Creswell Lane Extension
Opelousas, Louisiana 70570— **Map Location #4**
866-472-2477
www.evangelinedowns.com

Description: The racino has 80,000 square feet of entertainment including 1,700 slots, the Cajun Buffet, fine dining, 24-hour café and a raised centerpiece casino lounge with seating for 110. There is live quarterhorse racing in spring and fall and thoroughbred racing in summer. Simulcasting is offered all year.

Directions: From I-10 exit 103, take I-49 to exit 18. Turn right on Creswell. The entrance to the racino is on the left just past the Wal-Mart on the Creswell extension. RVs should park in the north lot. An RV park is planned in the future.

Riverboats — New Orleans Area

NOTE: Bally's in New Orleans was closed indefinitely after the 2005 hurricane. Before driving into Bally's, please contact the casino to confirm whether they have reopened or are planning to reopen.

Bally's Casino Lakeshore Resort
1 Stars & Stripes Boulevard
New Orleans, Louisiana 70126 — **Map Location #5**
504-248-3200 • 800- 57-BALLY
www.ballysno.com

Description: This small red, white and blue America-themed paddlewheeler on Lake Pontchartrain features 1,222 slots in all denominations, ten tables, a buffet and snack bar. Monthly tournaments are held for blackjack, craps and mini-baccarat.

Discounts: 15% off food and gift shop purchases for seniors. A bounce-back coupon for $10 of slot play will be mailed to new slot club members.

Directions & Parking: From I-10 exit 242, take Crowder Blvd north for one mile (Crowder ends here); then right on Hayne Blvd and get in the right lane for .4 mile. Cross the bridge, then make a U-turn 1,000 ft. after the bridge and double back to the casino. Follow tour bus signs to the front of the casino. Security will meet you there to assist with parking. RV parking is limited to 24 hours.

Boomtown Casino - Westbank
4132 Peters Road
Harvey, Louisiana 70058 — **Map Location #5**
504-366-7711 • 800-366-7711
www.boomtowncasinos.com

Description: A comfortable and roomy 30,000 square foot casino on three levels; 1,500 slots and video poker machines in a wide variety of styles and denominations, 22 pit/gaming tables on the main level and a seven-table poker room on the third level. There is a separate non-smoking area for slot players. Food venues include the Bayou Market buffet, Bayou Market Express for a quick snack and Pier 4 fine dining. An interesting display on the history of gaming and a few vintage slot machines can be viewed in the casino lobby.

Discounts: New slot club members receive a valuable FunPak with over $100 in coupons and a 50% coupon for the buffet.

Directions & Parking: The casino is about 12 miles from the interstate. From I-10 eastbound, take exit 234B; From I-10 westbound, take exit 234C. Cross the bridge and continue on elevated Westbank Expressway (US-90 West Business Route) for six miles. Exit at Manhattan Blvd – exit 6. Continue on ground-level Westbank Expressway middle lane (do not enter tunnel). Follow the blue casino signs. The expressway ends at Peters Road. Turn left and follow Peters Rd for 4.5 miles to the casino. The designated area for large vehicles is in the southeast corner of the parking lot. A courtesy shuttle is available.

Note: When on I-10 going past downtown, you may notice green signs reading "Casino Area." Those signs refer to the one land-based casino in the city, but it is not advisable to get off the interstate in this area. There is no parking for RVs in the downtown section and the narrow streets are not RV-friendly.

Treasure Chest Casino
5050 Williams Boulevard
Kenner, Louisiana 70065 — **Map Location #5**
504-443-8000 • 800-298-0711
www.treasurechestcasino.com

Description: The 1,900-passenger paddlewheeler located in Kenner (a suburb of New Orleans) has 900 slots on three decks – most are ticket in/ticket out. There are 16 pit/gaming tables – 30X odds on craps. The Texas (top) Deck has a separate Penny Parlor and a non-smoking area. Food venues include Treasure Island Buffet and Bobby G's for casual dining. Free nightly entertainment is featured.

Discounts: New Prime Rewards members receive a valuable coupon book after 30 minutes of slot play. Senior members of Prime Rewards, 50 and older, are eligible for monthly specials.

Directions & Parking: From I-10 exit 223, north on Williams Blvd (SR-49) for 1.5 mile to the casino on the shores of Lake Pontchartrain. RVs should park in the Ponchartrain Center lot. A courtesy shuttle runs between parking lots and the casino.

Riverboats — Baton Rouge

Casino Rouge
1717 River Road North
Baton Rouge, Louisiana 70802 — **Map Location #6**
225-381-7777 • 800-44-ROUGE
www.pngaming.com

Description: The 24-hour casino has 1,085 slots in denominations from 2¢ to $25, video poker, 31 pit/gaming tables and a separate high limit area. Food venues include Capitol Bistro Steakhouse, International Marketplace Buffet (which overlooks the Mississippi River) and Dockers Grill for a quick snack. Rhythms Lounge features live entertainment and has 17 TVs.

Discounts: New Club Rouge members who coin in $10 on the first visit will receive a $10 coupon in the mail within 14 days.

Directions & Parking: From I-10 exit 155 to I-110, exit at North St. This is an exit ramp from the left lane! Take North St for .6 mile, then right on River Road to the casino on the left. Free overnight parking is available in the lot along River Rd (next to railroad tracks). Security will assist with parking. A courtesy shuttle operates between the parking lot and the casino.

Note: The other Baton Rouge casino – Argosy – is docked one mile down river from Casino Rouge. But it is in a congested downtown area where streets are narrow and parking space is limited.

Riverboats — Lake Charles

Harrah's Lake Charles
507 North Lakeshore Drive
Lake Charles, Louisiana 70601 — **Map Location #7**
337-437-1500 • 800-977-PLAY
www.harrahs.com

Description: Two three-level casinos – The Star and The Pride – have 1,600 slots and 70 pit/table games. Both casinos have slots of all denominations on the first level. The Pride has 38 table games on Level Two; penny and nickel slots are on Level Three. The Star has video poker and 13 live action poker tables on Level Two; baccarat and pai gow on Level Three. Craps has 20X odds. The casino is open 24/7. Harrah's Festival of Food features seven choices: the buffet, a steakhouse, oriental restaurant, seafood specialty restaurant and two Cajun food venues. A jazz brunch is held every Sunday.

Discounts: Total Rewards members get $1 off the buffet. A $3.99 breakfast is featured at Pepper House Friday–Saturday, midnight–10am. Harrah's sponsors valuable seasonal promotions; ask about current offerings at the Total Rewards booth. Total Rewards points can be earned on the same card at all Harrah's properties throughout the country.

Directions & Parking: From I-10 east take exit 29; from I-10 west, take exit 30A. On weekends large vehicles must park in Lot C, the free park and shuttle lot across the interstate from the casino (parallel to the westbound lanes of I-10). On weekdays, RV parking is permitted in the casino parking lot at the west corner of the casino near the parking garage, if there is room. Overnight parking is permitted for self-contained vehicles.

To get to Lot C: From exit 30A, follow the access road for a mile all the way around under the bridge, then for another mile past the casino and follow signs to Lot C. From exit 29, follow the access road for .5 mile past the casino and follow the sign to Lot C. The shuttle bus runs continuously. There are phones in the bus stops in case you need to call the casino to inquire about the shuttle.

Isle of Capri Casino & RV Spaces – Lake Charles

100 Westlake Avenue
Westlake, Louisiana 70669 — **Map Location #7**
337-430-0711 • 888-475-3847
www.isleofcapricasino.com

Description: There are eight spaces with electric hookups in the parking lot adjacent to the 493-room hotel. The spaces are tight and there is no room to extend slideouts. Daily rate last year was $5 for the electric hookup and use of the hotel's fitness center and showers, located just steps away from the RV spaces. Advance reservations are accepted and are strongly suggested on weekends, as the RV spaces fill up fast. The 24-hour casino features more than 1,500 slots and about 60 pit/gaming tables aboard two 1,200-passenger paddlewheelers on Lake Charles. The Isle resort also includes four restaurants.

Discounts: IsleOne club members who are 50 or older can receive a free buffet if they earn 30 points or more on Monday, Wednesday or Friday.

Directions & Parking: From I-10 exit 27, the Isle of Capri can be seen from the interstate. Follow the green casino signs after exiting I-10. Free overnight RV parking is also available in the lot on the north side of the casino complex along the fence by the I-10 bridge.

Note: Delta Downs Raceway is located 20 miles west of Lake Charles. It features live thoroughbred and quarter horse racing, simulcasting daily and a slots-only casino.

Riverboats — Shreveport / Bossier City

Isle of Capri Casino Resort & RV Park – Bossier City
711 Isle of Capri Boulevard
Bossier City, Louisiana 71111 — **Map Location #8**
318-678-7777 • 877-465-3711
318-678-7661 (RV park)
www.isleofcapricasino.com

Description: The modern RV park has 32 level paved sites with water, electric, sewer, phone, cable TV and picnic tables. Showers, laundry facilities, vending and ice machines are in the clubhouse. Staff is on duty 24 hours. Last year's RV rates were $25 (plus tax) with the IsleOne card and $30 without a card. Early reservations are suggested. The tropical-themed casino on three levels has 1,100 slots, 30 gaming tables and three restaurants (one open 24 hours). The hotel has 530 rooms/suites.

Discounts: Stop at the IsleClub desk to get a coupon for buffet discounts.

Directions & Parking: From I-20 take exit 20A to Isle of Capri Blvd. Free parking is also available in the front lot when the RV park is full.

Boomtown Casino – Bossier City
300 Riverside Drive
Bossier City, Louisiana 71111 — **Map Location #8**
318-746-0711 • 866-462-8696
www.boomtowncasinos.com

Description: The western-themed riverboat casino has 1,200 slots from 1¢ to $100, on three levels and 36 gaming tables, including high limit areas. Food venues include the Cattlemen's Buffet, Circle R Ranch Steakhouse and a casual café. The hotel has 188 rooms/suites.

Discounts: Senior discounts include $2.99 breakfast on Wednesdays. Senior Day every Wednesday features slot tournaments and valuable coupons. There are also discounts available for slot club members at the buffet every day.

Directions & Parking: From I-20 take exit 19B. On entering the Boomtown complex go straight and turn left into the lot alongside the hotel. RV parking space is limited.

Horseshoe Casino Hotel – Bossier City
711 Horseshoe Boulevard
Bossier City, Louisiana 71111 — **Map Location #8**
318-742-0711 • 800-895-0711
www.horseshoe.com

Description: The 30,000 square-foot Vegas-style casino has 1,700 slots on three levels, 50 gaming tables and five restaurants, including Jack Binion's Steakhouse, the Village Square Buffet, an oriental restaurant, a café and deli. The hotel has 606 suites. A retail shopping concourse features upscale gift shops. A unique display in the lobby features $1 million in $100 bills.

Directions & Parking: From I-20 exit 19B turn left to the casino. Enter the casino complex and turn left at the first or second driveway into the RV lot. Overnight parking is permitted.

Sam's Town Shreveport
315 Clyde Fant Parkway
Shreveport, Louisiana 71101 — **Map Location #8**
877-429-0711
www.samstownshreveport.com

Description: Located on the Red River in downtown Shreveport, the 30,000 square-foot casino features slots, pit/gaming tables and a 514-room hotel on site. Restaurants include the International Buffet, Smokey Joe's Café, and William B's for steak and seafood.

Directions & Parking: From I-20 exit 19A, Spring St, go four blocks and turn right on to Fannin. RV parking is tight and limited. Spaces are available in the Expo Hall lot across from the casino.

Eldorado Casino Shreveport
451 Clyde Fant Parkway
Shreveport, Louisiana 71101 — **Map Location #8**
877-602-0711
www.eldoradoshreveport.com

Description: The casino offers over 1,400 slot machines in a variety of denominations, 68 pit/gaming tables and a spacious pavilion with five restaurants including a buffet, steakhouse and 50's style diner. The hotel has 403 suites.

Directions & Parking: From I-20 exit 19A, Spring St, proceed to Milam St, right on Milam to Clyde Fant Pkwy. Limited RV parking spaces are available. Pull up to the valet area and they will assist with parking.

Note: Harrah's Louisiana Downs featuring live quarter horse and thoroughbred racing is also located in Boosier City. It has a slots-only casino. Louisiana Downs is just off I-20 at exit 20; it can be seen from the westbound lanes of the interstate. Overnight parking is permitted.

Michigan

Michigan is known as "The Great Lakes State" where residents and visitors can enjoy 3,200 miles of Great Lakes shoreline. The 15 Indian casinos listed in this section are all RV-friendly. Ten are located in the Upper Peninsula, far from major population centers. Outdoor non-

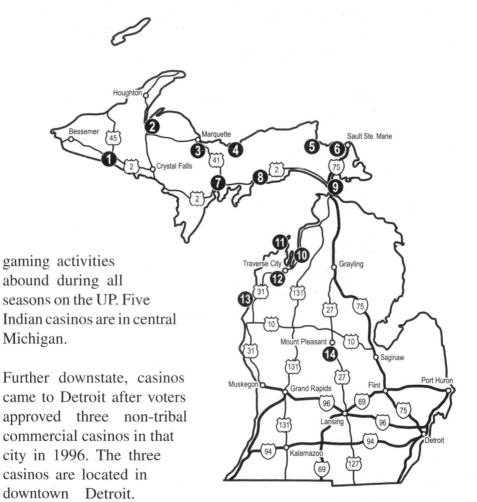

gaming activities abound during all seasons on the UP. Five Indian casinos are in central Michigan.

Further downstate, casinos came to Detroit after voters approved three non-tribal commercial casinos in that city in 1996. The three casinos are located in downtown Detroit. However, it is not advisable to take a motor home into the motor city. The casino facilities are in busy inner city areas with traffic congestion, many narrow, one-way streets and restricted parking. The multi-tiered garages at these casinos cannot accommodate large vehicles.

Upper Peninsula, page 112

Central Michigan, page 118

Upper Peninsula

Lac Vieux Desert Casino & RV Park
N 5384 US-45 North
Watersmeet, Michigan 49969 — **Map Location #1**
906-358-4226 • 800-583-3599
800-895-2505 (RV park)
www.lacvieuxdesert.com

Description: The facility, owned by the Lake Superior Chippewa Indians, includes a 76-room/suite hotel and an RV park. Located in the pristine forest land of the western UP, the RV park features 14 electric and water hookups. RV park registration is at the hotel. Last year's rate was $5 per night; the RV park is closed during winter months. The casino has more than 600 slots plus 21 pit/table games and a poker room (Thu–Sun). The resort also includes Katikitegoning Restaurant, featuring a different buffet every day of the week, snack bar and a 9-hole golf course.

Discounts: Various senior discounts, if 55 and older, are given on Tuesdays. Ask about them at the casino.

Directions: Located in the western UP, two miles north of the junction of US-2 and US-45 (about eight miles north of the Wisconsin border).

Two Ojibwa casinos in the northwest UP on Lake Superior are owned and operated by the Keneenaw Bay Indian Community:

Ojibwa Casino Resort & RV Spaces
797 Michigan Avenue
Baraga, Michigan 49908 — **Map Location #2**
906-353-6333 • 800-323-8045
www.ojibwacasino.com

Description: Located near Sandpoint Lighthouse on Keneenaw Bay, the casino features over 400 slots (denominations from 2¢–$5), 13 gaming tables, Bear's Den Restaurant and an eight-lane bowling alley. The facility is open 24/7 all year. There is a 40-room hotel and 12 full hookup RV spaces; last year's charge for full hookup was from $10.

Directions & Parking: From US-41 in Baraga, one mile west on M-38.

Ojibwa Casino & RV Spaces – Marquette
105 Acre Trail
Marquette, Michigan 49855 — **Map Location #3**
906-249-4200 • 888-560-9905
www.ojibwacasino.com

Description: The casino features over 300 slots and pit/gaming tables (including $1 blackjack). There is a snack bar.

Discounts: Monday specials are offered for seniors 55 and older.

Directions & Parking: From US-41 north at junction of US-41 and M-28 in Harvey, east on M-28 for four miles. RV parking with free electric hookups is available in the casino lot.

Kewadin Casino – Christmas
N 7761 Candy Cane Lane
Munising, Michigan 49862 — **Map Location #4**
906-387-5475 • 800-KEWADIN
www.kewadin.com

Description: Surrounded by the extraordinary natural beauty of the northern UP along the shores of Lake Superior, this casino is located just west of Munising. Open seven days a week 8am–3am, the casino features Vegas-style gaming, Frosty's Bar & Grill and the Northern Lights gift shop.

Discounts: Ask about senior specials offered every Wednesday from 8am to 7pm if 50+.

Directions & Parking: From I-75 exit 386, west on M-28 (a major east–west route in the UP) for approximately 2.5 hours. Free overnight parking is available for self-contained RVs.

Two affiliated casinos in Brimley – Bay Mills and Kings Club – are owned by the Bay Mills Native American Community. The Bay Mills Reservation on the UP north shore is noted for its captivating views and rich Native American history. The two casinos are located just four miles from one another and a free shuttle operates between them. Bay Mills has a modern RV park.

Bay Mills Resort Casino & RV Park
11386 West Lakeshore Drive
Brimley, Michigan 49715 — **Map Location #5**
906-248-3715 • 888-422-9645
www.4baymills.com

Description: The resort includes an RV park, open all year, and a 144 room/suite hotel. There are 76 shaded sites with full hookups, cable TV, picnic table and fire pit at the RV park. It includes showers, restrooms and laundry facilities and is within walking distance to the casino. 2005 daily RV rates were from $15. The casino has three signature restaurants, more than 500 slots, 15 gaming tables and a poker room open seven days. The 18-hole Wild Bluff championship golf course is also located at Bay Mills.

Discounts: A Fun Book is given with slot club membership. Wednesday is Senior Day from 8am–2pm with cash drawings and buffet discounts for seniors 60 and older.

Directions: From I-75 exit 386, west on M-28, then north into Brimley and west on Lakeshore Drive.

Kings Club Casino
12140 West Lakeshore Drive
Brimley, Michigan 49715 — **Map Location #5**
906-248-3700 • 888-422-9645
www.4baymills.com

Description: Affiliated with Bay Mills, the smaller casino has 7,400 square feet of gaming and a deli. Shuttle service operates between the two casinos.

Discounts: Seniors, 50 and older, receive discounts every Tuesday; ask for details.

Directions: From I-75 exit 386, west on M-28, then north into Brimley and west on Lakeshore Drive.

Kewadin Casino Hotel & RV Park – Sault Ste. Marie
2186 Shunk Road
Sault Ste. Marie, Michigan 49783 — **Map Location #6**
906-632-0530 • 800-KEWADIN
www.kewadin.com

Description: The resort includes a 320-room/suite hotel and a 75-space RV park with electric hookups. Open May through October, last year's daily rate at the RV park was $12. RV guests are invited to enjoy the hotel's indoor pool. The 37,000 square foot Vegas-style casino features over 1,000 slots, pit/gaming tables, poker room open Thu–Sun, restaurant, deli and sports bar. The Bawating Gallery has the largest collection of Woodland Indian art in the Midwest. Sault Ste. Marie is Michigan's oldest city and local attractions include the Agawa Canyon and the world-famous Soo Locks.

Discounts: RV park guests receive $5 in tokens from the Northern Rewards booth. Ask about senior discounts on Tuesdays if 50 and older.

Directions: From I-75 exit 392 (before the bridge to Ontario) turn right off the exit, then right at Mackinaw Trail (second light), then take an immediate left onto Three Mile Road. Left on Shunk Road and .5 mile to the casino.

Island Casino Resort & RV Park
W399 Highways 2 & 41
Harris, Michigan 49845 — **Map Location #7**
906-466-2941 • 800-682-6040
www.chipincasino.com

Description: The modern RV park has 53 paved sites with water and electric hookups, shower/laundry facilities, paved roads and a central dump. Last year's daily rate was $15. The park is open May through November. Shuttle service is provided from RV sites to the casino that has 970 slots, 24 pit/gaming tables and a poker room open Wed–Sun. Dining options include the Fireside Restaurant and the Coral Reef Grille. There is a 113-room/suite hotel on site. RV guests may use the resort amenities including an indoor pool with a unique heated sand beach. Thornbury's Creamery, located near the pool, has gourmet custard ice cream. Live entertainment is featured weekly in the lounge.

Discounts: Ask about incentives for slot club membership.

Directions: From Escanaba (on the northern shore of Lake Michigan), travel 13 miles west on Hwy-2 & 41 into Harris.

Kewadin Casino & RV Park – Manistique
S630W US-2 East
Manistique, Michigan 49854 — **Map Location #8**
906-341-5510 • 800-539-2346
www.kewadin.com

Description: The Kewadin Inn, about a mile west of the casino, has 40 motel rooms and 40 wooded RV sites with water and electric, central dump and laundry facility. RV guests are invited to use the indoor pool at the Inn. Free shuttle service is provided to the casino. Last year's daily rate was $18. The casino offers Vegas-style gaming in a hometown atmosphere. It has over 300 slots, nine gaming tables, Mariner's Cove Restaurant and Team Spirits Bar.

Discounts: Specials are offered for seniors, 50 and older, on Wednesdays 8am–7pm.

Directions & Parking: From I-75 exit 344B west on US-2 for 86 miles. The Inn and casino are located west of the Mackinaw Bridge. Free RV parking is available in the casino parking lot.

Kewadin Casino – St. Ignace
3039 Mackinac Trail
St. Ignace, Michigan 49781 — **Map Location #9**
906-643-7071 • 800-KEWADIN
www.kewadin.com

Description: The casino, open every day 24/7, has over 1,000 slots, Vegas-style gaming tables, poker room and the Market Square Buffet Restaurant. A new casino building is expected to open in summer, 2006.

Discounts: Northern Rewards players who are 50 and older, receive $5 in tokens on Thursdays from 7am–7pm.

Directions & Parking: St. Ignace is the gateway to the Upper Peninsula, near Mackinac Island and the Mackinac Bridge. From I-75 northbound, take exit 348, then left on to Mackinac Trail for two miles. From I-75 southbound, take exit 352, left on M-123, then right on Mackinac Trail for four miles. Ample parking is provided for RVs; overnight is OK.

Central Michigan

Victories Casino
1966 US-131
Petosky, Michigan 49770 — **Map Location #10**
231-439-9100 • 877-4-GAMING
www.victories-casino.com

Description: Nestled along the banks of Little Traverse Bay on eastern Lake Michigan, the casino features over 850 slots in all denominations and a variety of table games. The resort includes a full service restaurant, a deli and lounge with live entertainment. The casino is open daily 8am–4am.

Discounts: Ask about senior specials on Wednesdays and Sundays if 55 and older.

Directions & Parking: From I-75 southbound, (exit four miles after Mackinaw Bridge) take US-31 south for 35 miles to the junction with US-131. Casino is 2.4 miles on left. From I-75 northbound, take exit 282 to M-32 for 15 miles to US-31 north for 24 miles. Casino is on the right. RVs should use the lower lot on the south side of the casino.

Leelanau Sands Casino & RV Spaces
2521 N West Bay Shore Drive
Peshawbestown, Michigan 49682 — **Map Location #11**
231-271-4104 • 800-922-2946
www.casino2win.com

Description: Owned and operated by the Grand Traverse Band of Ottawa and Chippewa Tribes, the 72,000 square foot casino features slots of all denominations, Vegas-style gaming tables, poker room open seven days, Double Eagle Restaurant and the Sand Dollar Bar. It is open seven days a week 10am–2am, year round.

Discounts: Ask about specials for seniors, 55 and older, on Tuesdays.

Directions & Parking: From Traverse City, 20 miles north on M-22. The RV lot is across the street from the casino (next to the gas station). Electric hookups are $7 per night; go to the casino gift shop to pay for electric.

Turtle Creek Casino
7741 M-72 East
Williamsburg, Michigan 49690 — **Map Location #12**
231-267-9546 • 888-777-UWIN
www.casino2win.com

Description: The 29,000 square foot casino features slot machines from nickels to $10, table games, Misheekeh Restaurant and Creek Side Café. The casino is open 24 hours all year.

Directions & Parking: From Jct. US-131 & M-72 in Kalkaska, west on M-72 into Williamsburg. Enter the casino property and go to the lot on the far left side. Shuttle service is available to the casino.

Little River Casino Resort & RV Park
2700 Orchard Highway
Manistee, Michigan 49660 — **Map Location #13**
231-723-1535 • 888-568-2244
www.littlerivercasinos.com

Description: The resort includes a 100-room/suite hotel and a modern 46-space RV park. Open April through November, the RV park features water and electric at the sites, central dump, an outdoor pavilion with picnic area, a guest lounge with TV and laundry. The park is walking distance to the casino but shuttle service is also provided. RV park guests may use the hotel facilities: indoor pool/spa, sauna and fitness room. Daily RV rates were from $26 last year. The friendly casino features 1,200 slots, 30 table games and a six-table poker room. Three restaurants include fine dining, buffet and deli.

Discounts: Ask about one-free-day specials at the RV park. Senior discounts are offered at the casino on Wednesdays. Ladies Day and Men's Day specials are run seasonally.

Directions & Parking: Manistee is near the east shore of Lake Michigan. From US-131 (major north/south route) Cadillac exit, take M-55 west to junction with US-31, then north for 3.1 miles on US-31. Casino is on the left. Overnight parking is also permitted in the parking lot (no hookups); there is a $5 charge for use of the central dump.

Soaring Eagle Casino & Resort
6800 East Soaring Eagle Boulevard
Mount Pleasant, Michigan 48858 — **Map Location #14**
989-775-5777 • 888-7-EAGLE-7
www.soaringeaglecasino.com

Description: The sprawling resort has 210,000 square feet of gaming in two buildings with 4,700 slots, 55 pit/gaming tables and poker room open every day. A 511-room/suite hotel and three restaurants are on site.

Discounts: Half price breakfast buffet on Wednesdays for seniors 55 and over.

Directions & Parking: From US-127, take M-20 east (Pickard) for 1.2 miles. Turn right on to Leaton Road and follow signs to the RV parking lot. A large parking area is designated specifically for RVs. Shuttle service is provided to the casinos 24 hours.

Minnesota

Casinos in Minnesota are located throughout the state, many of them in the very heart of the "Land of the Lakes," where outdoor recreational activities abound. Virtually all Minnesota casinos have hotel accommodations and all are RV-friendly with comfortable campgrounds

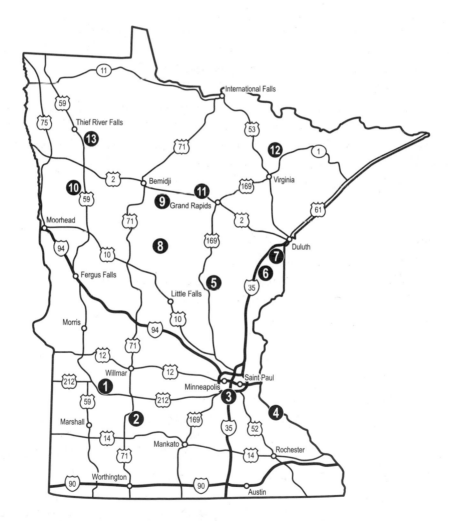

or parking facilities. Casino resorts in the southern part of the state are lavish entertainment destinations featuring large Vegas-style casinos and a variety of luxurious amenities.

Minnesota has had gambling since 1988 when the state's 11 Indian Tribes requested compacts to operate casinos with video games of chance. Later table games, blackjack and poker, were added, and the expansion of Minnesota's gaming sites continues.

Southern Minnesota, page 122

Northern Minnesota, page 127

Southern Minnesota

Prairie's Edge Resort Casino
5616 Prairie's Edge Lane
Granite Falls, Minnesota 56241 — **Map Location #1**
320-564-2121 • 866-293-2121
www.prairiesedgecasino.com

Description: Owned and operated by the Upper Sioux Community, the resort includes a convention center, 87-room hotel with indoor pool, whirlpool, sauna, fitness room and business center. The comfortable casino features 600 video slots and friendly dealers at eight blackjack tables with four and six-deck shoes. Restaurants include menu service at Cottonwood Café plus Meadows Buffet serving three meals daily and a champagne brunch on Sundays. The Firefly Lounge and Deli are located in the casino. A smoke-free slots area is located at the Prairie's Edge C Store.

Discounts: Senior discounts are given on Mondays if 55 and older. Players Club discounts at the gas station.

Directions & Parking: On Hwy-23 (three miles south of Granite Falls) turn east on to Hwy-274; then go one mile east on Prairie's Edge Lane to the casino. Free RV parking is available in the lot; overnight is OK.

Jackpot Junction Casino Hotel & RV Park
39375 County Highway 24
Morton, Minnesota 56270 — **Map Location #2**
507-644-3000 • 800-WIN-CASH
800-946-0077 (RV park)
www.jackpotjunction.com

Description: The Lower Sioux Indian Community owns and operates the resort that includes a hotel with 276 rooms/suites, indoor pool/spa, sauna, game room and fitness center. The RV park, open mid-April to mid-October, has 40 full hookup gravel sites. Most sites are back-in and somewhat tight for big rigs. Only four pull-thru sites are available and these are along the roadway. There are showers and a convenience store within walking distance. The RV park is walking distance to the casino. 2005 rates were $15 weekdays and $20 weekends. There are extra charges for RV guests who want to use the hotel amenities. The casino has 1,650 slots, 38 blackjack tables and a six-table poker room. The resort also includes five food venues and an 18-hole Rees Jones championship golf course with 7,100 yards of unique diverse terrain. There is a conference center at the resort as well as headline entertainment in the amphitheater on weekends and live entertainment in the lounge.

Discounts: Seniors 55 and older receive 25% off Wednesday lunch or dinner buffet. Daily gaming packages are offered to RV guests who have a Jackpot Express Club card.

Directions: From I-90 exit 73, take US-71 north to Jct. US-71/SR-19 & CR-2, then south on CR-2 for 1.25 miles.

Mystic Lake Casino Hotel & RV Park
2400 Mystic Lake Boulevard
Prior Lake, Minnesota 55372 — **Map Location #3**
952-445-9000 • 800-262-7799
www.mysticlake.com

Description: The casino resort includes a hotel and RV park. The hotel has 595 rooms/suites, indoor pool, whirlpool, sauna, fitness center, meeting rooms, convention center, live headline entertainment and an 18-hole golf course. The modern 122-space Dakotah Meadows Campground features full hookup sites, Tipi rentals, internet modem access, a group pavilion, fuel center and a self-serve RV car wash with catwalk. Last year's daily fees were from $30. The 24-hour casino has 4,000 slots and 64 blackjack tables. There is a high stakes blackjack room and a separate non-smoking slots section. Food venues include The Buffet, Ribbons Steakhouse for fine dining, the 24-hour Minnehaha Café and Gambler's Grille for deli fare. A second casino, Little Six, is located a half-mile from the Mystic Lake complex and has 587 slots and eight blackjack tables. Shuttle buses operate 24 hours throughout the resort complex. The famous Mall of America is nearby.

Discounts: A Fun Book is given to new slot club members.

Directions: Mystic Lakes is located 25 miles southwest of the Twin Cities. From I-35W exit 1, go west on CR-42 for nine miles, one mile south on CR-83 —or— From I-494 exit 10, take US-169 south (Townline Rd) for 6.5 miles, then CR-18 south for 3.4 miles to CR-42 west for three miles to CR-83 (Mystic Lake Dr) for one mile.

Treasure Island Resort Casino & RV Park

5734 Sturgeon Lake Road
Red Wing, Minnesota 55066 — **Map Location #4**
651-388-6300 • 800-222-7077
www.treasureislandcasino.com

Description: The casino resort is located near the Mississippi River and has an RV park and a 247-room hotel with indoor pool, fitness center and a game room. The RV park, open April 1–Oct. 31, has 95 pull-thru sites with full hookups. Last year's RV rate was $18; RV guests are invited to use the pool at the hotel. Boating and fishing are available nearby. The 24-hour Caribbean-themed casino features 2,500 slots, video poker, video roulette and 50 blackjack tables. Food venues include a buffet and fast food restaurant. Mississippi River cruises (dinner and sightseeing) are available nearby on weekends in season.

Discounts: Seniors, if 55 and older, receive a valuable coupon book on the first Wednesday of the month 10am–2pm.

Directions: The resort is located 40 miles southeast of the Twin Cities. From Jct. US-61 (at MP 99) and CR-18 go 2.6 miles north on CR-18, then follow casino signs for one mile on Sturgeon Lake Rd. Note: there are steep grades on CR-18.

Grand Casino Mille Lacs

777 Grand Avenue /US-169
Onamia, Minnesota 56359 — **Map Location #5**
320-532-7777 • 800-626-LUCK
www.grandcasinosmn.com

Description: On the shore of Lake Mille Lacs, the resort includes a 284-room hotel, a spacious Vegas-style casino and meeting rooms. The casino has 2,000 slots, including penny machines, video poker and progressives; 30 live blackjack tables include two, four and six deck games. There is a separate poker room and bingo. The four food venues include buffet, fine dining and a snack bar. Headline entertainment is featured on weekends. The Mille Lacs Indian Museum, located nearby, features extensive displays and exhibits dedicated to telling the story of the local band of Ojibwe. Also on site is a restored trading post.

Directions & Parking: Located about 90 miles north of the Twin Cities, take I-694 exit 29 to US-169 north. Just past Onamia, US-169 becomes a two-lane road. Stay on US-169 for eight more miles to the casino on the west side of the highway. RVs should follow signs to the designated area for oversized vehicles. Security will assist with parking. Overnight parking is OK.

Grand Casino Hinckley & RV Park
777 Lady Luck Drive / Highway 48
Hinckley, Minnesota 55037 — **Map Location #6**
320-384-7777 • 800-472-6321
www.grandcasinosmn.com

Description: The RV resort has 222 full hookup RV sites with patios and cable TV and 100 chalets, modern one or two bedroom cabin units with cable TV, kitchen and maid service. Included at the RV resort are heated pool/spa, shuffleboard, horseshoes, game room and playground. Last year's daily rates were from $16 for RV sites and $39–$99 for chalets. The hotel and the Grand Hinckley Inn on property also provide accommodations. Kids Quest child care center and a video arcade are located in the hotel. There is a free pet kennel. Food venues at the resort include a buffet restaurant, steakhouse, fine dining fast food and snack bar. The casino has 2,144 slots, 28 live blackjack tables, poker room and bingo. Entertainment is featured daily and live outdoor concerts are held during summer months. The 18-hole Grand National Golf Course is located at the resort. 24-hour shuttle service runs throughout the resort.

Directions: From I-35 exit 183, east on SR-48 for one mile to the resort.

Black Bear Casino & Hotel
1785 Highway 210
Carlton, Minnesota 55718 — **Map Location #7**

218-878-2327 • 888-771-0777
www.blackbearcasinohotel.com

Description: The casino features 1,200 slots, video craps and 12 blackjack tables. Restaurants include a buffet, fine dining, and a 24-hour café. Bingo is held seven days a week. The casino is open 24/7. The 218-room hotel has a skywalk to the casino.

Discounts: Senior specials are offered on Mondays and Tuesdays for 55+.

Directions & Parking: From I-35 exit 235, the casino is on the west corner of Hwy-210, visible from the southbound lanes of the interstate. Designated RV spaces are in the back parking lot and free overnight parking is permitted.

Northern Minnesota

Northern Lights Casino
6800 Y Frontage Road N.W.
Walker, Minnesota 56484 — **Map Location #8**
218-547-2744 • 800-252-7529
www.northernlightscasino.com

Description: The casino features 924 slots from 1¢ to $1, video poker and progressives with high payoffs. The blackjack area has 12 tables with limits from $3 to $200; tournaments are held every Wednesday. The casino also has a poker room, a pretty North Star Buffet and the Little Star snack bar. A 90-foot dome above the casino simulates star constellations. The modern 105-room hotel and conference center also houses the Dancing Fire Restaurant with menu service from morning to night.

Directions & Parking: The casino is located at the junction of Highways 371 and 200 on the south shore of Lake Leech (175 miles north of the Twin Cities). RVs should park in the west lot, within walking distance to the casino. Overnight parking is permitted for RVs. There are free electric hookups.

Palace Casino Hotel & RV Spaces
6280 Upper Cass Frontage Road
Cass Lake, Minnesota 56633 — **Map Location #9**
218-335-7000 • 877-9-PALACE
www.palacecasinohotel.com

Description: The 30,000 square-foot casino features over 550 slots including progressives, poker and keno, six blackjack tables and The River poker room. It has a restaurant and snack bar and is open 24 hours daily. Bingo is held 7 days a week. There are 25 RV spaces with free electric hookups for overnight parking plus a dump station and fresh water. The hotel has 60 rooms/suites.

Directions & Parking: From I-35 exit 250, go west on US-2 into Cass Lake. There is a large casino sign on US-2, westbound lane. Go north on Hwy-75 for 1.3 mile. The free electric hookups are first-come, first-serve.

Shooting Star Casino Hotel & RV Park
777 Casino Boulevard
Mahnomen, Minnesota 56557 — **Map Location #10**
218-935-2701 • 800-453-STAR
www.starcasino.com

Description: Located on White Earth Indian Reservation, the resort has a 350-room hotel and a 47-site RV park. RV sites are open from May 1–Oct 1 and last year's daily rates were from $19. RV guests may use the amenities at the hotel including a spacious indoor pool and hot tub in an atrium, fitness room and an arcade. The casino features 1,300 slots, 20 blackjack tables, a poker room and a non-smoking gaming area. Weekly blackjack and poker tournaments are featured. Bingo is held on weekends. Food venues include Biindigaan Buffet, Whispering Winds for casual dining, Reflections for fine dining and Delites Deli. Monthly specials are featured at the restaurants. There are two lounges with live entertainment. Headline concerts are held on weekends in the event center.

Directions: From I-94 exit 60, take US-59 north to Mahnomen. Free overnight parking for RVs is permitted in the overfill lot designated for buses.

White Oak Casino
45830 US Highway 2
Deer River, Minnesota 56636 — **Map Location #11**
218-246-9600 • 800-653-2412
www.whiteoakcasino.com

Description: The 11,000 square-foot casino, known as the "Best Little Casino in Minnesota" has 306 slots, video poker and two blackjack tables, a full service bar, gift shop and snack bar.

Discounts: A free Fun Book is given on Tuesdays for seniors 50 and older; Fun Books are available for people under 50 on Thursdays.

Directions & Parking: The casino is located directly on US-2, five miles northwest of Grand Rapids and 2.2 miles west of Deer River. There is limited RV space in the parking lot. Overnight RV parking is permitted. The RV area is within walking distance to the casino.

Fortune Bay Resort & Casino & RV Park
1430 Bois Forte Road
Tower, Minnesota 55790 — **Map Location #12**
218-753-6400 • 800-992-7529
www.fortunebay.com

Description: The resort has 34 sites with electric and water, central dump and rest room/showers located in the parking area. Last year's RV fee was $14 and RV guests should register at the hotel. RV guests may use the heated pool/spa at the 116-room hotel. The resort is on Lake

Vermilion with excellent boating and freshwater fishing; boat rentals are available. The resort also has an 18-hole golf course. The 24-hour casino has 1,100 slots, a non-smoking slots area, 12 blackjack tables, video keno, video poker and a poker room. It has a buffet restaurant, deli in the casino, sports bar and entertainment.

Discounts: Senior specials are offered on Mondays and Thursdays for 55 and older.

Directions: Located about 80 miles northwest of Duluth, from I-35 exit 237, take Hwy-33 north for 19 miles to US-53 north for 46 miles to Hwy-169 north for 17.2 miles to CR-77 north for 1.6 mile, then east on CR-104 for .7 mile. Free overnight parking is not provided for RVs. RVs are required to pull into the fee-pay area.

Seven Clans Casino – Thief River Falls
County Road 3
Thief River Falls, Minnesota 56701 — **Map Location #13**
218-681-4062 • 866-255-7848

Description: The 16,000 square-foot, 24-hour casino has 760 slots and eight blackjack tables with bets from $2–$200. The 151-room hotel features Native American art in the lobby. There is a large indoor water park/pool, an arcade and gift shop. The Seven Clans Buffet is open morning to night. There is a snack bar at the water park and a 24-hour Triple 7 Malt Shop in the casino.

Discounts: Specials every Tuesday for 55+.

Directions & Parking: From I-94 exit 60, take US-59 north or 27 miles, then right on CR-3 for .7 mile — or — From I-29 exit 161 in ND, east on SR-1 and cross the Red River into Minnesota; continue east for 28 miles into Thief River Falls, then south on US-50 for eight miles to CR-3 east for .7 mile. Free overnight parking for RVs is available in the east lot.

Mississippi

Despite the hurricane damage it sustained in 2005, Mississippi is still known as the "Casino Capitol of the South." It is home to more than a dozen riverboat casinos on the Mississippi River as well as one land-based casino, Pearl River.

The spectacular Pearl River Resort, located in east-central Mississippi, is the state's largest casino resort. It is owned and operated by the Mississippi Band of Choctaw Indians.

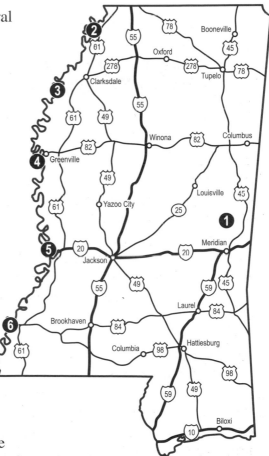

Riverboat casinos located in Tunica County (in the northwestern corner of the state) as well as others in various locations along the banks of the Mississippi River survived undamaged by the hurricane season of 2005. The nine casino resorts in Tunica County make that region the most popular "casino hopping" destination in the state.

Unfortunately, casinos in Biloxi, Gulfport and Bay St. Louis along the Gulf Coast were forced to close as a result of the massive hurricane damage to their facilities in August, 2005. These include:

- In Biloxi: Isle of Capri Casino, Casino Magic, Grand Casino, Beau Rivage Resort, Boomtown Casino and Imperial Palace.
- In Gulfport: Copa Casino, and
- In Bay St. Louis: Casino Magic.   .

Three Biloxi casinos re-opened by January, 2006. All the other Gulf Coast casinos plan to re-open on various dates throughout 2006.

Land-Based Casino, page 133

Map   *Casino*
1   Pearl River Resort

Tunica County Riverboat Resorts, page 133

Map   *Casino*
2   Grand Casino Tunica & RV Park
2   Hollywood Casino Tunica & RV Park
2   Sam's Town Hotel & Gambling Hall & RV Park
2   Resorts Tunica
2   Bally's Casino Tunica
2   Sheraton Casino & Hotel
2   Horseshoe Casino & Hotel
2   Gold Strike Casino
2   Fitzgerald's Casino / Hotel

Casinos On The Mississippi River, page 139

Map   *Casino*
3   Isle of Capri Casino - Lula
4   Lighthouse Point Casino
5   Isle of Capri Casino, Hotel & RV Park - Vicksburg
5   Ameristar Casino Hotel - Vicksburg
5   Horizon Casino
5   Rainbow Casino
6   Isle of Capri Casino & Hotel - Natchez

Land-Based Casino

Pearl River Resort
Highway 16 West
Philadelphia, Mississippi 39350 — **Map Location #1**
601-650-1234 • 866-44-PEARL
www.pearlriverresort.com

Description: Two Las Vegas-style casinos fill 175,000 square feet of gaming including 5,000 slots, 150 pit/gaming tables and poker room. Tournaments and specials are featured throughout the week in the poker room. The Silver Star and Golden Moon Hotels & Casinos are across the street from one another and are connected by a covered sky bridge with moving sidewalks, ideal for those who want to casino-hop from one to the other. Shuttle service is provided to other attractions in the large resort that includes 15 restaurants, two award-winning golf courses, outdoor and indoor pools, retail shops, a 15-acre Geyser Falls Water Theme Park with swimming facilities, a wave pool, 12 water slides and more. In the evening, there is a free outdoor musical with laser imagery, water screen projections, dancing fountains and fireworks.

Discounts: New Players Club members get a free buffet if they sign up before 5pm, Monday through Thursday.

Directions: From I-20 exit 109, north on Rt-15 for 30 miles to Hwy-16, then west for 3.8 miles. The central Mississippi resort is 35 miles northwest of Meridian and 72 miles northeast of Jackson. Free overnight parking is available for RVs in the Golden Moon east lot.

Tunica County Riverboat Resorts

Tunica County, in northwest Mississippi, is home to nine casino resorts and ranks as the nation's third most popular destination for gaming. All casino resorts have hotels and three also have RV parks. The riverfront resorts are nestled near the cotton fields in the fertile Mississippi River

Delta, where the weather is mild and pleasant year round. Although the casino resorts are some distance from one another, a shuttle service has three buses circulating from one casino to another continuously from 10am–11pm on weekdays and to 3am on weekends. Popular country and western stars are always among the headliner entertainment featured at virtually all resorts throughout the year. The *Tunica Queen*, a paddlewheeler that day-cruises on the river, is a popular local non-gaming activity.

The largest casino in Tunica County, Grand Casino Tunica, is on Old Highway 61 north of the other resorts. The Grand has a modern 200-space RV park.

On Casino Center Drive, Gold Strike, Horseshoe and Sheraton are clustered together, walking distance from one another. Fitzgerald's and Bally's are a short shuttle hop away.

On Casino Strip Blvd, Sam's Town, Hollywood and Resorts are within walking distance of each other and all are RV-Friendly. Both Sam's and Hollywood have modern RV parks. An 18-hole golf course is located at the Hollywood Resort.

Directions to the Tunica County Resorts:

- From I-55 in Memphis, TN, take exit 7 to US-61 (a four-lane highway) south for 20 miles.
- From I-55 in MS, take exit 280 (Hernando) to SR 304, then west on 304 (a two-lane scenic route) for 19 miles to US-61.

Note: All the Tunica County casinos are in the town of Robinsonville, MS. The casino resorts with full-service RV parks – Grand, Hollywood and Sam's – are listed first in the following section.

Grand Casino Tunica & RV Park
13615 Old Highway 61 North — **Map Location #2**
662-363-2788 • 800-946-4946
www.grandtunica.com

Description: The Grand is the world's largest dockside casino resort. It has a 200-space RV park and a hotel with over 1,300 rooms/suites. The modern RV park has paved sites with full hookups, cable TV and pool, shuffleboard, horseshoes, a lodge, playground, and laundry. Last year's rates were from $17 on weekdays and $19 on weekends. The 140,000 square-foot casino at the Grand has 3,200 slots and 109 gaming tables. The poker room has 14 tables, including five non-smoking. The resort includes eight restaurants, spa and salon and an 18-hole championship golf course.

Discounts: Good Sam and AARP discounts are honored. RV rally groups are always welcome and a group rate is available for ten or more.

Directions: Located on Old US-61, 2.1 miles north of SR-304.

Hollywood Casino Tunica & RV Park
1150 Casino Strip Resorts Boulevard — **Map Location #2**
662-357-7700 • 800-871-0711
www.pngaming.com

Description: Hollywood has a 494-room/suite hotel and a modern RV park. The RV park has 123 paved patio sites with full hookups, cable TV, phones at the sites and laundry; heated pool/spa and game room at the hotel. Last year's rates were from $12, with a seven-day maximum stay. The Hollywood-themed casino has 1,500 loose slots, 44 pit/gaming tables, a six-table poker room, high limit slots area and a separate high limits blackjack room. An interesting collection of Hollywood memorabilia is displayed at the casino. Among its three restaurants is the signature Fairbanks Steakhouse. The River Bend Scottish-links golf course is challenging for golfers of all levels.

Discounts: Slot Club members get a 10-15% discount at the restaurants and gift shop.

Directions: From Jct. US-61 and SR-304, west on SR-304 for six miles. Dry camping is permitted in the lot behind the hotel.

Sam's Town Hotel & Gambling Hall & RV Park

1477 Casino Strip Resorts Boulevard — **Map Location #2**
662-363-0711 • 800-456-0711
www.samstowntunica.com

Description: Sam's Town has an RV park and 850-room hotel. The modern 100-site RV park offers full hookups, phone and cable TV, BBQ grill and picnic table at each site and paved park roads with security patrols. RV guests are invited to use the hotel's pool and fitness center. Daily trash pickup and a free courtesy shuttle between the RV park and the casino are included. Last year's RV rate was $9.99 per night. The casino has two floors of gaming featuring over 1,500 slots, 47 gaming tables and a separate poker room. Restaurants include The Great Buffet, Corky's BBQ Buffet, Smokey Joe's Restaurant and Twain's Casual Fine Dining. Live entertainment is featured every weekend.

Discounts: Ask about special promotional rates when checking into the RV park. RV rallies are welcome and should be booked through the convention sales department.

Directions: From Jct. US-61 and SR-304, west on SR-304 for six miles. Free overnight parking is available on the west side of the main lot.

Resorts Tunica

1100 Casino Strip Boulevard — **Map Location #2**
662-363-7777 • 866-706-7070
www.resortsint.com

Description: A comfortable casino with over 1,400 slots in all denomination from 1¢ up, 23 gaming tables and a poker room. The hotel has 200 rooms/suites. Three restaurants include the Resorts Buffet and a 24-hour café. There is free live entertainment on weekends. An 18-hole golf course is adjacent to the resort.

Directions & Parking: From Jct. US-61 & SR-304, go west for six miles on SR-304 (Casino Strip Blvd). RVs may park in the lot behind the casino, follow signs for the dry camping area. A free dump station and fresh water are available on site.

Bally's Casino Tunica
1450 Bally's Boulevard — **Map Location #2**
662-357-1500 • 800-382-2559
www.ballysms.com

Description: The Western-themed casino has over 1,300 slots and 47 tables, including $3 blackjack, 50¢ roulette and 25¢ craps. The Maverick Room caters to high stakes players. The hotel has 243 rooms/suites; a reasonably priced 24-hour buffet features five cooking stations. Bally's is home to Tunica's only comedy club.

Discounts: Players Club members who are 55 and older receive 50% off daily buffets. There is a free buffet on Thursdays for ladies who are club members.

Directions & Parking: From US-61, left on Casino Center Drive and follow signs to Bally's. RVs should park in the east lot. Overnight parking is OK.

Sheraton Casino & Hotel
1107 Casino Center Drive — **Map Location #2**
662-363-4900 • 800-391-3777
www.caesars.com/Sheraton/Tunica

Description: A 33,000 square foot casino with over 1,300 slots and 45 pit/gaming tables and 144-room/suite hotel. Food venues include Louie's Steakhouse, Reno's Café and the Big Kitchen buffet, an international flavor fest.

Directions: From US-61, follow signs to Casino Center Drive. RV parking is not allowed.

Horseshoe Casino & Hotel
1021 Casino Center Drive — **Map Location #2**
662-357-5500 • 800-303-7463
www.horseshoe.com

Description: This upscale hotel has over 500 rooms/suites and the casino has more than 1,500 slots and 60 tables. A unique poker room features a striking wall mural depicting a 19th century poker table, flanked by the "Poker Hall of Fame: Legends of the Game" and "World Series of Poker: Gallery of Champions." Notable poker tournaments are held at the Horseshoe. Restaurants include Jack Binion's Steak House, Yasmin's Asian, Café Sonoma and Village Square Buffet. Live entertainment is presented weekly.

Directions & Parking: From US-61 follow signs to Casino Center Drive. RVs should park on the east side of the building.

Gold Strike Casino
1010 Casino Center Drive — **Map Location #2**
662-357-1111 • 888-24K-PLAY
www.goldstrikemississippi.com

Description: The 50,000 square foot casino includes over 1,400 slots, 50 table games and three restaurants, a food court and Starbucks. A poker room is on the upper level. The hotel has 1,200 rooms/suites.

Directions: From US-61 follow signs to Casino Center Drive.

Fitzgerald's Casino / Hotel
711 Lucky Lane — **Map Location #2**
662-363-5825 • 800-766-LUCK
www.fitzgeraldstunica.com

Description: An Irish-themed casino on two floors, with over 1,200 slots and 34 pit/gaming tables plus a sports pub with multiple TVs. Restaurants include Limerick's Steakhouse, Castle Court Buffet and Shamrock Café, open 24 hours. The hotel has 577 rooms/suites.

Discounts: The NY Steak and eggs special is on the menu all day at the Shamrock Café. The casino also has a daily breakfast buffet at a discounted price.

Directions & Parking: From CR-304 (Casino Strip Blvd) follow signs to Fitzgerald's Blvd. RVs should use the south lot. Free overnight parking is permitted.

Casinos On The Mississippi River

South of Tunica County, casinos along the Mississippi include:

- In Lula, MS — Isle of Capri,
- In Greenville, MS — Bayou Caddy's and Lighthouse Point,
- In Natchez, MS — Isle of Capri, and
- In Vicksburg, MS — Isle of Capri, Ameristar, Rainbow and Horizon.

Isle of Capri Casino – Lula
777 Isle of Capri Parkway
Lula, Mississippi 38644 — **Map Location #3**
662-363-4600 • 800-789-LUCK
www.isleofcapricasino.com

Description: The 65,000 square foot casino features 1,550 slots and 41 gaming tables, plus the Isle signature restaurants. The hotel has 177 rooms/suites.

Discounts: Ask about specials for seniors 50 and older on Tuesdays and Thursdays.

Directions & Parking: From I-55 (in Memphis, TN) exit 7, take US-61 south for 58 miles, then US-49 west to the river. RVs are welcome to park in the lot adjacent to the casino.

Lighthouse Point Casino
199 North Lakefront Road
Greenville, Mississippi 38701 — **Map Location #4**
662-334-7711 • 800-878-1777

Description: A 22,000 square foot casino with slots and pit/gaming tables on an actual paddlewheel boat. The Bayou Caddy's Jubilee Casino is located next to Lighthouse Casino and a shuttle operates between the two.

Discounts: Membership in the Wild Bunch Seniors Club gives you a free Hot Seat Wednesday entry.

Directions & Parking: From I-55 exit 185, west on US-82 for approximately 90 miles, through the town of Greenville to Broadway. North on Broadway to the second traffic light, then left to the levee. The two casinos are visible from the top of the levee. RVs may park in the Lighthouse lot and use the shuttle for the Jubilee.

Vicksburg, Mississippi

A note about RV parking in Vicksburg: RVs going into Vicksburg are advised to stay at the Isle of Capri RV Park. Access roads into the parking lots at all four casinos have steep grades down and there is the possibility your vehicle may bottom-out while trying to enter or exit the parking lots. Because of the generally unsafe and crowded conditions for large vehicles in the main casino lots, parking for RVs or semis is prohibited.

Isle of Capri Casino, Hotel & RV Park – Vicksburg
3990 Washington Street
Vicksburg, Mississippi 39180 — **Map Location #5**
601-636-5700 • 800-THE-ISLE
www.isleofcapricasino.com

Description: The RV park has 67 paved patio sites with full hookups, cable TV and phones at the sites, heated pool/spa and laundry. Last year's rates were from $15. The Isle of Capri Casino with 750 slots and 28 pit/gaming tables is located across the street and down the hill from the RV park (not walking distance). A shuttle bus runs every 30 minutes between the casino and the RV park. The hotel connected to the casino has 61 rooms. There are two restaurants and one is open 24 hours.

Discounts: The RV park gives a 20% discount to IsleOne Club card-holders. Ask about current casino discounts for seniors 50+.

Directions: From Jct. of I-20 and Washington St (exit 1A), north .3 mile on Washington St. Turn right into the park.

Ameristar Casino Hotel – Vicksburg
4146 Washington Street
Vicksburg, Mississippi 39180 — **Map Location #5**
601-638-1000 • 800-700-7770
www.ameristarcasinos.com

Description: The picturesque red and white riverboat features over 1,300 slots and 40 gaming tables on two levels. It is located at I-20 exit 1A just north on Washington St. Oversize vehicle parking is prohibited.

Horizon Casino
1310 Mulberry Street
Vicksburg, Mississippi 39180— **Map Location #5**
601-636-DICE • 800-843-2343

Description: The casino and hotel are located about two miles upriver from I-20 adjacent to downtown Vicksburg. It is not advisable to drive an RV into the area – streets are narrow and there is no room to park large vehicles. However, if you are staying at the Isle of Capri RV Park and want to drive a dingy or tow vehicle up to Horizon Casino, you'll find some 700 slots, 40 pit/gaming tables and a separate poker room aboard the paddlewheel riverboat. Tournaments are held weekly in the poker room.

Rainbow Casino
1380 Warrenton Road
Vicksburg, Mississippi 39182 — **Map Location #5**
601-636-7575 • 800-503-3777
www.rainbowcasino.com

Description: The 35,000 square foot casino features over 900 slots, 16 gaming tables and The Blind Dog poker room with tournaments and game specials. The Rainbow Buffet is open for breakfast, lunch and dinner. The adjacent motel has 85 rooms. Rainbow is located off I-20 exit 1A, 1.5 miles south of the interstate.

Discounts: Players Club members get $1 off on buffets. Ask about discounts for seniors 50 and older.

Isle of Capri Casino & Hotel – Natchez
53 Silver Street
Natchez, Mississippi 39120 — **Map Location #6**
601-445-0605 • 800-772-LUCK
www.isleofcapricasino.com

Description: The riverboat casino has over 500 slots plus pit/gaming tables and the Isle's signature restaurant on the top level. The hotel has 147 rooms.

Directions & Parking: From Jct. US-61 and US-84 in Natchez, go west on US-84 for two miles, then north on Canal for .7 mile to the parking lot at D.A. Biglane St. Turn right into the parking lot. Call the casino for a pickup. Overnight parking is permitted in the lot at D.A. Biglane St.

Missouri

Voters in Missouri approved riverboat gambling in 1992. Thus they became the fifth state to have riverboat casinos. All boats must remain dockside. Missouri has an unusual "loss limit" in force at all casinos in the state. When boarding a riverboat casino, patrons are required to present an ID and receive a slot club card. The card is used to track that

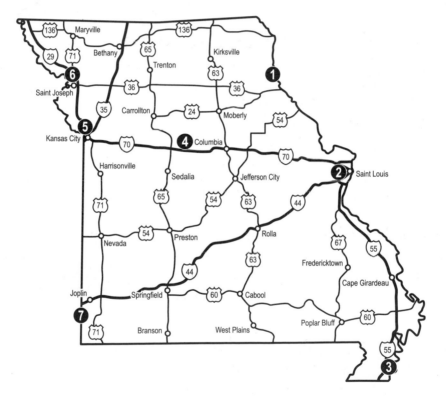

person's chip and slot token purchases. Individuals are not allowed to play more than $500 in any two-hour period. Efforts to repeal the loss limit were unsuccessful during the 2005 state legislative session.

Most casinos in Missouri are not open 24 hours – their hours of operation are noted in each listing. Some casinos charge admission. The ten riverboats listed here are convenient to a nearby interstate or major highway and offer adequate free parking for motor homes. Terrible's

Mark Twain Casino in La Grange has electric hookups in designated RV parking spaces, and Casino Aztar in Caruthersville has an RV park.

One Indian casino in Seneca, Missouri is located near the Oklahoma border and is operated by the Eastern Shawnee Tribe.

Eastern Missouri, page 144

Central Missouri, page 147

Western Missouri, page 148

Eastern Missouri

Terrible's Mark Twain Casino / RV Parking
104 Pierce Street

La Grange, Missouri 63448 — **Map Location #1**
573-655-4770 • 866-454-5825
www.terribleherbst.com

Description: This RV-friendly casino has seven full hookup parking spots with electric hookups in an adjacent lot. Last year's fee: $5 per night. A refundable deposit is required. The casino has over 500 slots from penny to $25 plus 16 pit/table games. Weekly slot and blackjack tournaments are featured. The casino is open 8am–2am/4am (Fri–Sat). Admission is free. Food venues include Clemens Café, a full service restaurant, and Saloon 777 that has fast food.

Discounts: 10% off food on Monday and Wednesday for seniors 55 and older.

Directions: From I-70 take Hwy-61 north for 100 miles to La Grange —or— From I-72 take Hwy-61 north 30 miles to La Grange. The casino is located on the south end of La Grange on Old Hwy-61, which is now Route B.

Ameristar Casino St. Charles
1260 South Main Street
St. Charles, Missouri 63301 — **Map Location #2**
636-949-4300 • 800-325-7777
www.ameristarcasinos.com

Description: The 2,000-passenger barge remains dockside and is open 8am–5am/24 hrs. (Fri–Sat). The casino features 3,300 slots and video poker. All machines are ticket-in/ticket-out. There are 95 pit/gaming tables, 10X odds on craps, and a live poker room with 14 tables, open seven days. Eight food venues include a steakhouse, 24-hour diner and buffet restaurant. There is a small slots-only, non-smoking area on the second floor.

Directions & Parking: From I-70 exit 229B, go to the first traffic light, turn right on to Riverbluff Dr for .5 mile to Main St. For RV parking, DO NOT cross the bridge. Turn right on Main St and go to the first left into the oversize vehicle parking lot under the bridge. The RV parking lot is under the main entrance to the casino. Shuttle service is provided. Please notify Security if you plan to stay overnight.

Harrah's St. Louis
777 Casino Drive
Maryland Heights, MO 63043 — **Map Location #2**
314-770-8100 • 800-HARRAHS
www.harrahs.com

Description: Voted the best casino in St. Louis, Harrah's offers over 110,000 square feet of Vegas-style gaming in the Mardi Gras and Island casinos, dockside on the Missouri River. The casino includes over 2,500 slots and video poker machines, 70 table games and a separate poker room. The resort includes a 291-room/suite hotel and five restaurants including Town Square Buffet Riverfront and Range Steakhouse. Casino hours are 8am–5am/24 hrs (Fri–Sat). Admission is free.

Directions & Parking: From I-70 exit 231A, south on Earth City Expressway for 1.5 miles to the third stoplight. Parking for large vehicles is on the south side of the lot. Overnight is OK; please check in with Security.

Casino Aztar & RV Park
777 East Third Street
Caruthersville, Missouri 63830 — **Map Location #3**
573-333-6000 • 800-679-4945
800-679-4945 (RV park)
www.casinoaztarmo.com

Description: The 875-passenger sternwheeler is docked on the Mississippi River in southeast Missouri. There is a 27-space full hookup RV park with wireless Internet throughout, cable TV, 24-hour security and shower and laundry facilities. A nature trail offers great Mississippi River views from dawn to dusk. Last year's rate was $20; RV check-in is at the gift shop in the pavilion between noon and 10pm. Other times, Security will assist with parking.

The casino has over 650 slots in all denominations, and table games including blackjack, poker, roulette, craps and three-card poker. There is a poker room, open daily from 10 am, on the top deck with four tables featuring seven-card stud, Texas Hold 'Em and Omaha poker. The first deck is smoke free. Corky's BBQ restaurant, open daily from 11am, features a buffet on Saturday evenings. Sidelines sports bar is open daily. Casino hours are 9am–3am/6am (Fri–Sat).

Discounts: RV park discounts include $3 for Good Sam and $3 off with a Players Club card. Wednesday is Senior Day in the casino.

Directions & Parking: From I-55, exit 19 (Hayti), east on Hwy-84 for 4.4 miles, then continue straight ahead on 3rd Street for .8 mile. Channel 15 on a CB radio may be used to call for the casino shuttle. If coming in from I-40 in Tennessee, take exit 79 and follow US-412 west for 44.7 miles to I-155 west. Stay on I-155 for 15 miles to the Mississippi River; after crossing the river take exit 6 in Missouri and go north on SR-84/ Ward Ave for two miles. Stay on Ward Ave (when SR-84 turns) and continue for another 1.5 miles through the city of Caruthersville to 3rd St. Turn right on 3rd St to the casino and follow signs to the RV park.

Central Missouri

Isle of Capri Casino
100 Isle of Capri Boulevard
Boonville, Missouri 65233 — **Map Location #4**
660-882-1200 • 800-THE-ISLE
www.isleofcapricasino.com

Description: The 28,000 square-foot casino features over 900 slots, 35 pit/table games and three signature restaurants: Farradday's, Calypso's Buffet and Tradewinds Marketplace. There is an historic display in the pavilion. Hours are: 8am–5am/24hrs (Fri–Sat). Admission is free.

Discounts: The Paradise 50 Club offers benefits for seniors.

Directions & Parking: From I-70 exit 103 (Hwy-B), go north three miles and turn left on Morgan St, go one-half mile to the casino. RVs are welcome in the parking lot. Overnight is OK; check in with Security.

Western Missouri

Ameristar Casino Hotel – Kansas City
3200 North Ameristar Drive
Kansas City, Missouri 64161 — **Map Location #5**
816-414-7000 • 800-499-4961
www.ameristarcasinos.com

Description: This friendly casino has over 2,700 slots from pennies to high limits, video poker, 100 gaming tables and the largest poker room in the Midwest featuring regularly scheduled tournaments. Food venues include the 24-hour Falcon Diner, Horizons Buffet, a steakhouse, oyster bar, deli and a food court. There is a 188-room/suite hotel and an 18-theater movie complex on site. The casino barge remains dockside on the Missouri River and is open 8am–5am/24 hrs (Fri–Sat).

Discounts: A buffet discount is offered for slot club members.

Directions & Parking: From I-435 in Missouri, exit 55, go east for one mile on Rt-210, then south on Ameristar Dr. Parking spaces are available for RVs. Overnight parking is permitted for self-contained vehicles.

Argosy Casino
777 N.W. Argosy Parkway
Riverside, Missouri 64150 — **Map Location #5**
816-746-3100 • 800-900-3423
www.pngaming.com

Description: The 62,000 square-foot casino features over 1,700 coinless slot and video poker machines and 40 pit/gaming tables on a single level. It is open 8am–5am/24hrs (Fri–Sat). There are five food and beverage areas. Live entertainment is featured in the Casino Stage Bar. A 256-room hotel is expected to open in 2006.

Discounts: Ask about discounts on select days if 55 or older.

Directions & Parking: From I-70, turn right at Broadway to Riverside Hwy-9 and follow casino signs. RVs should use the west end of the lot. Overnight is OK.

Harrah's North Kansas City
One Riverboat Drive North
North Kansas City, Missouri 64116 — **Map Location #5**
816-472-7777 • 800-HARRAHS
www.harrahs.com

Description: Docked on the Missouri River, the barge has a 215-room/suite hotel and 60,000 square feet of slots, video poker, pit/gaming tables and poker room in two gaming areas (Island Casino and Mardi Gras Casino). Food venues include a steakhouse, buffet, deli and café. Hours are 8am–5am/24hrs (Fri–Sat). Admission is free.

Discounts: Buffet discounts for Total Rewards members.

Directions & Parking: From I-35 exit 6A east on Hwy-210 (Armour Rd) for one mile, then south on Chouteau Trafficway to Harrah's on the right —or— From I-435 exit 55A to Hwy-210 west for approximately two miles to Chouteau Trafficway, then south for .25 mile. There is a designated parking area for large vehicles; ask Security for directions and notify them if you plan to stay overnight.

Isle of Capri – Kansas City
1800 East Front Street
Kansas City, Missouri 64120 — **Map Location #5**
816-855-7777 • 800-946-8711
www.isleofcapricasino.com

Description: The Caribbean-themed casino aboard a dockside paddlewheeler on the Missouri River has over 1,100 slots and 25 pit/table games. Food venues include Farraddays fine dining every evening, Calypso Buffet daily breakfast, lunch and dinner, Tradewinds Marketplace open 24 hours and Island O'Aces for snacks and ice cream. Hours are 8am–5am/24hrs (Fri–Sun). Admission is free.

Discounts: Food discounts are extended on Thursdays to slot club members who are 50 and older. Free Paradise 50+ slot tournaments are featured.

Directions & Parking: From I-35 exit 4B, the casino is on Front St. RVs should park in the west lot which is connected to the casino by a walkway. Check in with Security if you plan to stay overnight.

Terrible's St. Jo Frontier Casino
777 Winners Circle
St. Joseph, Missouri 64501 — **Map Location #6**
816-279-5514 • 800-888-2946
www.terribleherbst.com

Description: The 600-passenger paddlewheeler docked on the Missouri River has slots and tables plus three restaurants. It is located 55 miles north of Kansas City. Hours are 8am–2am/4am (Fri–Sat). Admission is free.

Discounts: Senior citizens, 55 and older, receive 2-for-1 breakfast buffet on Wednesdays.

Directions & Parking: From I-29 exit 43, take I-229 north for seven miles to Highland Avenue exit, then west on Highland Ave. There is a designated parking area for RVs. Check in with Security if you plan to stay overnight.

Border Town Casino
130 West Oneida
Seneca, Missouri 64865 — **Map Location #7**

918-666-1126 • 800-957-2435
www.bordertownbingo.com

Description: Owned and operated by the Eastern Shawnee Tribe, there are two separate casino buildings open 24/7. The main building has 500 slots, video poker, and bingo seven days a week. The Turfside Room features off track betting of up to 20 pari-mutuel race tracks daily, 10am–12:30am. Family dining is available at the Country Kitchen Restaurant from 6am–10pm and fast food concessions are open 24 hours. The annex building features a poker room, pit/table games plus slots and video poker.

Directions & Parking: The casino is located on the Missouri/Oklahoma border. Directions from Missouri and Oklahoma follow.

From Missouri: From I-44 exit 11, go south on US-71 for 16 miles, then west on US-60 for 11 miles to SR-43. Go north on SR-43 for one mile into Seneca; after crossing the railroad tracks, take the first left on to Oneida St and go one-half mile to the casino.

From Oklahoma: From I-44 exit 302 (Afton/Fairland), take US-60 east for 27 miles to SR-43 north for one mile; after crossing the railroad tracks, turn left on Oneida St and go one-half mile to the casino.

RVs should park on the west side of the lot parallel to the roadway. Free overnight parking is available; please check in with Security.

Montana

Montana has limited gambling in effect. But this state's legalized gambling is definitely not Vegas-style "gaming." Traveling through the state you'll see scores of "casino" signs. But the typical "casino" in Montana is a relatively small establishment with up to 20 video gaming devices. The only games allowed are video poker, keno, bingo and live poker. The maximum bet is $2.

There are literally hundreds of "casino" locations throughout the state. Although they call themselves casinos, they really aren't. Generally, they consist of a small row of machines at a gas station, laundromat, truck stop, bar, tavern or club. Most only have the video poker and keno machines and some have live poker tables frequented by locals.

Big Sky country is not Big Casino country. You won't find Vegas-style slots or pit/table games in the state and certainly no lavish casino resorts.

RVers looking for a place to blacktop boondock in Montana should be very cautious and selective. In many cases, the so-called casinos are small and do not have parking lot security. We do not recommend overnight parking at any of these Montana establishments.

Nevada

The Nevada Legislature legalized most forms of gambling in the state in 1931, and for nearly 50 years afterward, it was the only state where you could go to casinos. The gaming industry in Nevada struggled until after World War II when the prosperity of post-war America started a boom. Then, casinos with lavish hotels, entertainment and restaurants became the norm for Las Vegas, Reno and other locations throughout Nevada.

Today Nevada still reigns as King Casino, with nearly 200 casinos throughout the state – all near or adjacent to interstates and major highways. RVers are welcomed warmly at most casinos in the state. The Nevada section highlights the following "casino hopping" destinations:

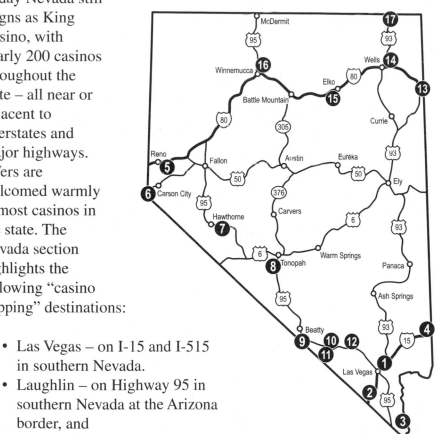

- Las Vegas – on I-15 and I-515 in southern Nevada.
- Laughlin – on Highway 95 in southern Nevada at the Arizona border, and
- Reno – on I-80 in western Nevada near the California border.

Also included are some of the RV-friendly casinos along Interstates 15 & 80 and other major highways in the state.

Las Vegas For The RVer

Even though RVers can now enjoy casinos in many parts of the country, Las Vegas, Nevada remains the premier gaming destination. But the Vegas area can be overwhelming. The sheer volume of casinos, restaurants and entertainment venues make it difficult to decide how to spend your time during your Las Vegas visit.

In Las Vegas it is highly recommended you stay at an RV park. As in any large metropolitan area, there will be safety and security concerns when motor homes are left unattended in areas generally open to the public. Las Vegas can be crowded and congested and – since 9/11 – security is heightened. The best strategy in Vegas is to check into a full service RV park and use shuttles, public transportation or your dingy or tow vehicle to get around town. Although there are lots of fine RV parks and campgrounds in Las Vegas – consistent with the theme of this book – in the Vegas section we feature only those RV parks directly connected to and owned by a casino: Circusland (the only RV park on the Strip); California (downtown) and Arizona Charlie's, and Sam's Town (on Boulder Highway). At these four RV parks, you have the advantage of full hookups in a park that is within walking distance to the casino.

Discounts in Las Vegas

Just as Vegas is the casino capitol of the country, it is also the casino discount capitol. Look for discount coupons in the free visitors' guides found on brochure racks all over town. You can even start collecting your Vegas discount coupons by checking out the free guides and brochures on racks at the state welcome center or at other stops along the way into Las Vegas.

Also, be sure to ask about specific casino discounts or coupon books when you join the Players Club at the casinos where you prefer to play.

Some of the free shows in Las Vegas include:

- *Rio Casino*: Masquerade Show in the Sky, spectacular high-energy Carnival production six times daily beginning at 3:30pm.

- *Bellagio*: Synchronized laser lights and music shows at the fountains in front of the casino every half hour during the day and every 15 minutes evenings.
- *Treasure Island*: Buccaneer Bay Sea Battle live action show at the pirate ship outside the casino four times daily beginning at 7pm.
- *MGM Grand*: Showcasing the lions at numerous viewing areas in the Grand Lion Habitat located inside the resort's Strip entrance starting at 11am daily.
- *Caesar's Palace*: Statues come alive during a seven-minute show at the Festival Fountains every hour on the hour in the Forum Shops Mall below the casino.
- *Circus Circus*: Acts featuring clowns, acrobats, jugglers, tightrope walkers and more, perform continuously daily from 11am to midnight.
- *Venetian*: Life-size puppets, magicians, stilt-walkers and living statues vie for your attention all day in St. Mark's Square. Accompanied by musicians, they perform in five shows daily.
- *Sam's Town*: A water and laser show daily at 2, 6, 8 and 10pm in the waterfall area of the indoor park.
- *Tropicana*: AirPlay, a high-flyin' variety show at 11am, 1, 3, 5, 7 and 9pm daily.
- *Downtown Area*: The Fremont Street Experience, a one-of-a-kind light & sound computer generated show in the sky every hour nightly from 7pm.

"Casino Hopping" On the Strip

The famed Las Vegas "Strip" consists of 3+ miles along Las Vegas Boulevard where you'll find some of the most fabulous casinos in the world showcased in lavish, bigger-than-life themed resorts. There is always something new in Vegas...new shows, new casinos, newly expanded or refurbished facilities. Some you won't want to miss include:

- At the north end: Stratosphere, Circus Circus, Sahara, Stardust, Westward Ho, Riviera and Frontier,

- In the heart of the Strip: Treasure Island, Venetian, Mirage, Harrah's, Imperial Palace, Flamingo, Barbary Coast, Caesars Palace, Bellagio, Bally's, Paris, Planet Hollywood and the new, spectacular Wynn Resort,
- At the south end: New York-New York, MGM Grand, Monte Carlo, Tropicana, Luxor, Excalibur and Mandalay Bay, and
- Just off the Strip: Hard Rock, Tuscany, Terrible's, Palms, Rio and Palace Station.

The newest addition on the Strip is the Wynn Las Vegas Hotel Casino, a $2.7 billion mega resort on 192 acres, mid-Strip. Its centerpiece is a 150-foot tall mountain with a five-story waterfall that cascades into a three-acre man-made lake. The resort also includes the only 18-hole golf course on the Strip, effectively replacing the old Desert Inn course that once occupied the site.

The Las Vegas Monorail is a convenient way to get from one end of the Strip to the other. There are seven monorail stations (running north to south) at: Sahara Ave & Paradise Rd, Las Vegas Hilton, Convention Center, Harrah's/Imperial Palace, Flamingo/Caesars Palace, Paris/Bally's and MGM Grand. The best monorail value is the one-day unlimited pass that allows you to get on and off at each station as many times as you like during a 24-hour period during operational hours (8am–midnight). With your monorail pass and a comfortable pair of walking shoes you can see all the sights on the Strip. Be sure to pick up a copy of the Monorail magazine at the station.

Before venturing out to the Strip, check out the free visitor guides found on brochure racks all over town. These guides feature current shows, special events, dining guides and detailed schedules for the free shows listed above. The *Today in Las Vegas* guide has a handy "easy to locate it" map on the inside of the front cover. Detailed information in the visitor guides will be helpful as you plan your excursions to the Strip. "Casino hopping" adventures in Vegas can take you to more than 30 glitzy casinos along Las Vegas Blvd. So, familiarize yourself with the area beforehand, plan your day and enjoy the Strip!

Las Vegas Area, page 159

Casinos with an RV park

Casinos on I-15 (south of Las Vegas), page 163

"Casino Hopping" in Laughlin, page 164

Casinos on I-15 (northeast of Las Vegas), page 166

Reno, The Biggest Little City..., page 169

RV Resorts in Verdi, page 172

Map	Casino
5	Boomtown Hotel, Casino & RV Park
5	Gold Ranch Casino & RV Resort

Carson City Area, page 173

Map	Casino
6	Carson Nugget
6	Pinon Plaza Casino Resort & RV Park
6	Carson Valley Inn & RV Park

Western Nevada (on US-95), page 175

Map	Casino
7	El Capitan Resort Casino
8	Tonopah Station & RV Spaces

Death Valley Region - near the CA/NV border, page 176

Map	Casino
9	Burro Inn Motel, Casino & RV Park
10	Longstreet Inn, Casino & RV Park
11	Saddle West Casino & RV Park
11	Terrible's Lakeside Casino & RV Park
12	Indian Springs Casino & RV Park

Northern Nevada Along I-80, page 178

West Wendover, NV

Map	Casino
13	Montego Bay Casino and RV Park
13	State Line Nugget Casino
13	Peppermill Inn & Casino
13	Rainbow Hotel Casino

Wells, NV

Map   Casino
14   Four Way Bar/Café & Casino
14   Lucky J's Casino

Elko, NV

Map   Casino
15   Gold Country Motor Inn & RV Park
15   Red Lion Inn & Casino
15   Commercial Casino
15   Stockman's Hotel & Casino

Winnemucca, NV

Map   Casino
16   Model T Hotel, Casino & RV Park

Jackpot, NV

Map   Casino
17   Cactus Pete's Resort Casino & RV Park
17   Barton's Club 93
17   Horseshu Hotel and Casino

Las Vegas Area

Casinos with an RV park

Circus Circus & KOA RV Park
2880 Las Vegas Boulevard
Las Vegas, Nevada 89109 — **Map Location #1**
702-734-0410 • 800-634-3450
800-562-7270 (RV park reservations)
www.circuscircus.com

Description: Circusland, on the north end of the Strip, has 400 paved full service sites, swimming pool & jacuzzi/sauna, playground, laundry facilities, pet runs and convenience store. Free circus acts run daily from 11am–midnight. Seasonally adjusted rates range from $19 to $60. The adjacent 24-hour Circus Circus casino has 109,000 square feet of gaming, nine restaurants, live circus acts and a carnival midway. Also featured is Adventuredome, an indoor themed amusement park with roller coaster, motion machines, log flume ride and children's rides and amusements. A People Mover monorail takes visitors to all areas of the Circus Circus complex.

Discounts: The KOA discount is the only one honored at the RV park.

Directions: From I-15 Sahara exit, east .2 mile on Sahara, cross the overpass, to South Bridge Lane, then south .1 mile to the rear entrance.

Boulder Highway - the Other Strip

Another major thoroughfare in Las Vegas is Boulder Highway. But casino hopping on the Boulder Strip is done by car, since casinos there are not within walking distance from one another.

Two casinos on the Boulder Strip that have modern RV parks are:

Arizona Charlie's Casino & RV Park – Boulder
4575 Boulder Highway
Las Vegas, Nevada 89121 — **Map Location #1**
702-951-9000 • 800-970-7280 (RV park)
www.azcharlies.com

Description: The RV park has easy access off the Boulder Strip. It has 239 paved full hookup sites, phones at the sites, shuffleboard, horseshoes, a picnic area, dog run, workout facilities and heated pool & spa. Last year's rates were $20–$26; with weekly and monthly rates available. A walkway leads to the casino that has slots and video poker, live pit/table games, 24-hour bingo and three restaurants, including a 24-hour café. The hotel has 300 rooms.

Discounts: FMCA discount is given at the RV park. The restaurant features a $2.49 steak & eggs special. Senior citizens, 55 and older, receive 10% off the buffet.

Directions: From Jct. I-515/93/95 exit 70, south 1.1 mile on Boulder Hwy.

Sam's Town Casino Resort & RV Park
5111 Boulder Highway
Las Vegas, Nevada 89122 — **Map Location #1**
702-456-7777 (Casino) • 702-454-8055 (RV park)
800-634-6371 (RV park reservations)
www.samstown.com

Description: The modern park on Boulder Highway has 287 full service sites, heated pool/spa, phones at sites and laundry facilities. Free shuttle service to the Strip and downtown casinos operates from 10am–11pm daily. Last year's RV rate was $24. The 100,000 square feet of casino gaming includes 2,700 slots, 40 pit/table games, poker room with nine tables, sports book, live keno and bingo. The Sam's Town complex includes a 650 room/suite hotel, 56-lane bowling center, movie complex and six restaurants – one is open 24 hours. A free laser light and water show is presented nightly.

Directions: From I-515 (93/95S), exit 68, go east on Tropicana Ave for 1.5 miles, then north on Boulder Hwy for .7 mile to Sam's Town RV Park entrance on the right. The lot for truck parking and RV dry camping is located on the other side of the casino building, at the corner of Flamingo and Perry. Security must be notified if you plan to stay overnight.

Downtown Casino Hopping

A dozen casinos are located in the downtown Fremont/ Ogden /Casino Center section of Las Vegas: Jack Binion's Horseshoe, California Hotel,

El Cortez, Fitzgerald's, Four Queens, Fremont, Gold Spike, Golden Gate, Golden Nugget, Lady Luck, Las Vegas Club, Main Street Station and Plaza. Most are located along the pedestrian mall known as "The Fremont Street Experience," offering another opportunity for casino hopping in Vegas. A free computer generated sound and light show takes place each night 90 feet in the sky over Fremont Street.

California Hotel, Casino & RV Park
12 Ogden Avenue
Las Vegas, Nevada 89101 — **Map Location #1**
702-385-1222 (Casino) • 800-713-8933 (RV park)
www.thecal.com

Description: The RV park located on Main Street, half a block from both California and Main Street Station, has 93 paved full hookup sites and 24-hour security. RV guests may use the pool and other amenities at the California Hotel. Last year's rates were $12–$15. RV guests should pull into a site, then register at the Main Street Station hotel front desk. The 35,000 square-foot California Casino has four restaurants and is walking distance to Fremont Street.

Directions: From Jct. I-15/93/95, east for .5 mile on US-93/95, then one block south on Casino Center Blvd, two blocks west on Stewart, then one block north on Main St. Register at the Main Street hotel desk.

Las Vegas Suburbs

Casinos located in the suburbs tend to be smaller facilities patronized by locals. Southeast of Las Vegas, ten casinos are in Henderson and one in Boulder City; three casinos can be found in North Las Vegas, five miles north of the Strip. The largest of the suburban casinos are: Sunset Station and Fiesta Casino (both can be seen from I-515) in Henderson and Cannery Casino and Fiesta Casino in North Las Vegas.

Casinos on I-15 (south of Las Vegas)

Primm Resorts & RV Park
I-15 at milepost 1
Primm, Nevada 89019 — **Map Location #2**
702-383-1212 • 800-FUN-STOP
www.primadonna.com

Description: The walled RV park has 197 full hookup sites (157 are pull thrus), laundry, swimming pool and playground. It is adjacent to a complex of three casinos. Last year's rate was $15. Casino hopping among the facilities is made easy by train shuttles that run from Buffalo Bill's to Primm Valley Resort to Whiskey Pete's. Buffalo Bill's has the rides: roller coaster, water slides and log flume and a movie theater. Al Capone's car and Bonnie & Clyde's "death" car are on display at Whiskey Pete's. All casinos are open 24 hours daily and have the full range of slots and pit/gaming tables plus more than a dozen food venues from fast food to full service restaurants.

Discounts: FMCA discount is honored at the RV park. Coupons are available in all brochure racks.

Directions: Located on I-15 at the California/Nevada state line.

Jean Nevada Casinos
I-15 at milepost 12
Jean, Nevada 89019 — **Map Location #2**
702-477-5000 • 800-634-1359
www.stopatjean.com

Description: Two friendly casinos are adjacent to I-15: Gold Strike on the northbound side and Nevada Landing on the southbound side. Both feature Las Vegas gaming; food venues include nine restaurants plus fast food. A shuttle runs between the casinos.

Discounts: $1.99 breakfast specials are offered in both locations.

Discount coupons are available at the hotel.

Directions & Parking: From I-15 take exit 12. Both casinos have large parking lots where overnight parking is permitted for self-contained RVs.

"Casino Hopping" in Laughlin

Laughlin is nestled in the Colorado River Valley where Nevada, Arizona and California meet. The City by the River has a special appeal...in Laughlin visitors can enjoy a slower-paced, pleasant casino hopping hiatus. There are 11 Vegas-style casinos, ongoing live entertainment, more than 60 restaurants, a museum, bowling center, boutiques, spas, salons plus many water sports and activities. Sightseeing on the Colorado River aboard the USS Riverside tour boat is a popular non-gaming activity. When you arrive in Laughlin, pick up a copy of *Laughlin Entertainer*, a free weekly publication that will give you information about current happenings and discounts around town. More than five million people visit Laughlin annually.

People who enjoy casino-hopping on foot will welcome the pretty walkway along the river where they can stroll along the picturesque river and stop at nine casinos along the way. For those who prefer to ride, there is a water taxi that goes from casino to casino on the river side and a city bus that runs along Casino Drive. Both are fee-pay transportation.

Accommodations in Laughlin: All casinos in town have hotels. There are two full-hookup RV Resorts in Laughlin: Riverside is the only RV Resort on Casino Drive and Avi Resort is located several miles south of town. For RVers looking to boondock, Harrah's has a designated RV parking lot and shuttle service is provided to the casino.

Don Laughlin's Riverside Resort & RV Park
1650 South Casino Drive
Laughlin, Nevada 89029 — **Map Location #3**

702-298-2535 • 800-227-3849
www.riversideresort.com

Description: The city itself is named after Don Laughlin, owner of the Riverside Resort, who settled there in 1966. His terraced RV park has a lovely view of the mountains. It features 840 full hookup spaces, laundry and showers. RV guests may use the two swimming pools and other amenities at the hotel. A climate controlled enclosed walkway connects the RV park with the casino; 24-hour shuttle service is provided. Last year's rates were from $20. The casino has over 1,700 slots; live gaming includes blackjack, poker, craps, roulette and bingo. Dozens of rare antique slot machines from Don Laughlin's private collection are on display in the casino. Also included at the resort are a 34-lane bowling center and a Western Dance Hall featuring live country bands. There is river access for boating and fishing from the resort.

Directions: Laughlin is located 100 miles south of Las Vegas. From Jct. of US-95 & SR-163, east for 19.9 miles on SR-163 to Casino Drive, then south for .4 mile.

Avi Resort & Casino
10000 Aha Macav Parkway
Laughlin, Nevada 89029 — **Map Location #3**
702-535-5555 • 800-430-0721 • 800-AVI 2 WIN (Reservations)
www.avicasino.com

Description: Avi is known for its spectacular beach, the largest along the banks of the Colorado River with views of the Mohave Valley. The hotel has 455 rooms. The RV park has 260 full service sites, pool, laundry, pavilion, lounge, beach and boat launch. Shuttle service is provided to the casino. 2005 RV rates were $19–$30. Recreation at the resort includes swimming, boating, canoeing, kayaking, fishing and an 18-hole golf course. The 25,000 square foot casino has over 800 slots and live table games including craps, 21, roulette, three-card poker, etc. Also included at the resort are kids quest and eight movie theaters.

Directions: The Avi is south of the rest of the Casino Drive casinos.

From I-40, River Road cutoff, which becomes Needles Hwy, north for 14 miles to Aha Macav Pkwy. Follow Avi signs.

Other casinos (listed from north to south) on Casino Drive include:

Flamingo Laughlin
1900 South Casino Drive — 702-298-5111 • 800-352-6464

Edgewater Hotel & Casino
2020 Casino Drive — 702-298-2453 • 800-677-4837

Colorado Belle Hotel/Casino & Microbrewery
2100 South Casino Drive — 702-298-4000 • 800-477-4837

Ramada Express Hotel Casino
2121 South Casino Drive — 702-298-4200 • 800-243-6846

Pioneer Hotel & Gambling Hall
2200 South Casino Drive — 702-298-2442 • 800-634-3469

Golden Nugget Laughlin
2300 South Casino Drive — 702-298-7111 • 800-950-7700

River Palms Resort Casino
2700 South Casino Drive — 702-298-2242 • 800-835-7904

Harrah's Laughlin Casino
2900 South Casino Drive — 702-298-4600 • 800-427-7247

Casinos on I-15 (northeast of Las Vegas)

Four casino resorts are located within a mile of the interstate in Mesquite – two at exit 120 and two at exit 122. They offer a variety of gaming and non-gaming activities. In addition to Vegas-style casinos, there are two 18-hole golf courses, health spas, a bowling center, movie theaters, live entertainment nightly and ten restaurants (some open 24 hours). Mesquite is 77 miles northeast of Las Vegas at the Arizona border. There are hotels and RV Resorts in Mesquite. In addition, there are provisions for free RV parking at Mesquite's casinos.

CasaBlanca Hotel, Casino, Golf, Spa & RV Park
950 West Mesquite Boulevard
Mesquite, Nevada 89027 — **Map Location #4**
702-346-7259 • 800-459-7529
800-896-4567 (RV park)
www.casablancaresort.com

Description: The resort includes an RV park with 45 paved sites with full hookups and patios, pool/spa and phones at the sites. 2005 RV rate was $15 with a seven-day maximum stay. There is a 540-room hotel on site. The 24-hour casino has over 700 slots and 26 pit/gaming tables. The resort also includes an 18-hole championship golf course and a world-class co-ed health spa offering massages, facials and mud treatments. Live lounge entertainment is featured nightly.

Directions: From I-15 exit 120, east for .1 mile. The resort is visible from the interstate. The parking lot for dry camping is east of the hotel building.

Oasis Resort Casino, Golf, Spa & RV Park
897 West Mesquite Boulevard
Mesquite, Nevada 89027 — **Map Location #4**
702-346-5232 • 800-21-OASIS
800-621-0187 (RV park)
www.oasisresort.com

Description: Oasis is the largest hotel in Mesquite and its RV park has 77 paved sites with full hookups, phones and patios, heated pool/spa and laundry. Daily RV rate in 2005 was $12.50 with a 14-day maximum stay. The 34,000 square-foot casino has Vegas-style slots, pit/gaming tables, live $100,000 keno and is open 24 hours. The resort features an 18-hole golf course, wagon trail rides, miniature golf, a go-cart track, shotgun sports club, health club/spa and live entertainment in the lounge nightly.

Discounts: 2-for-1 breakfast and lunch buffets are offered Sundays and Thursdays.

Directions: From I-15 exit 120, east .5 mile on I-15 Business Route.

Virgin River Hotel, Casino & Bingo
100 North Pioneer Boulevard
Mesquite, Nevada 89027 — **Map Location #4**
702-346-7777 • 800-346-7721
www.virginriver.com

Description: The resort features a 700-room hotel and a 49,000 square-foot casino, open 24 hours, bingo daily, live keno, 24-lane bowling center and four movie theaters.

Directions: From I-15 exit 122, north for .25 mile on the exit road. The casino is visible from the interstate. Free overnight parking is permitted for self-contained vehicles.

Eureka Casino & Hotel
275 Mesa Boulevard
Mesquite, Nevada 89027 — **Map Location #4**
702-346-4600 • 800-346-4611
www.eurekamesquite.com

Description: Open 24 hours, the 31,000 square-foot casino has the full complement of slots and live gaming tables and two restaurants.

Directions & Parking: From I-15 exit 122, Eureka is visible from the north side of the interstate. The large parking lot behind the 76 Gas Station is designated for trucks and RVs and is walking distance to both Virgin River and Eureka casinos. Boondocking is permitted.

Reno, The Biggest Little City...

Reno's famed landmark is the glitzy arch over Virginia Street proclaiming, "Reno – The Biggest Little City in the World." The arch was first built in 1899 and it was illuminated in 1928. The town of Reno was founded as a station on the Central Pacific Railroad in 1868 and was incorporated in 1903, named for General Jesse Reno, a Union general who was killed in the Civil War. Reno is located near the California border along I-80. Two Reno area casino resorts have RV parks: the Reno Hilton, closest to downtown, and Bordertown in North Reno. There are ten casinos in downtown Reno – eight toward the north side of Virginia St and two on South Virginia St. If you are coming to Reno with an RV, it is recommended you stay at an RV park and use your dinghy or tow vehicle to drive to the downtown Reno casino-hopping experience. As with any busy and congested downtown area, it is not wise (and in most places not permitted) to boondock at the downtown casinos.

Bordertown Casino RV Resort
19575 Highway 395 North
Reno, Nevada 89506 — **Map Location #5**
775-972-1309 • 800-443-4383
800-218-9339 (RV park)
www.bordertowncasinorv.com

Description: The high desert mountain resort has 50 paved and grassy sites with patios and tables, water, electric, dump station, and laundry facilities. It is open all year. Last year's rates were $15–$25. Maximum stay is 21 days. The casino has blackjack, video poker, slots, two restaurants and a gift shop.

Discounts: FMCA discount is honored at the RV park. Ask at the casino about a free Fun Book.

Directions: From I-80 & US-395, north on US-395 for 17.5 miles to the CA/NV border, exit 83. Go a quarter mile on Frontage Road.

Reno Hilton Casino Resort & RV Park
2500 East Second Street
Reno, Nevada 89595 — **Map Location #5**
775-789-2000 • 800-648-5080
775-789-2147 (RV park)
www.koa.com

Description: The closest casino RV park to downtown Reno is KOA at the Reno Hilton. It has 174 paved and gravel sites with full hookups, laundry facilities and a convenience store. RV guests are invited to use hotel amenities including swimming pool/spa, 50-lane bowling center, health club, shopping mall, golf driving range and ten restaurants. Open all year, RV rates in 2005 were $24–$69 (extra charge for pull thrus). The 100,000 square-foot casino is the largest in Reno and is within walking distance of the RV park. Other major Reno casinos are on Virginia Ave in downtown Reno, a short drive from this RV park.

Directions: From Jct. I-80 (exit 15) & US-395, south on US-395 for one mile to Glendale Ave (exit 67), then east on Glendale.

In all, there are ten casinos in downtown Reno. They are listed here from north to south as they are located on Virginia Ave. Many are walking distance from one another.

Circus Circus— Free circus acts. More than 1,500 slots from 1¢ to $5. Pit/table games.

Silver Legacy— Automated mining machine above casino floor. Over 2,000 slots, table games on 85,000 sq. ft.

Eldorado— ten restaurants, eight themed bars, microbrewery, in-house coffee roasting. 76,000 square feet of gaming.

Fitzgeralds— Irish themed casino. Loose $1 slots, second floor keno lounge, three restaurants.

Golden Phoenix— Formerly Flamingo Reno. Benihana Steak House, Golden Palace Chinese restaurant, espresso bar.

Club Cal-Neva— Multiple gaming floors, $1 minimum bet on craps and roulette, five restaurants.

Harrah's— More than 1,300 slots and table games on 53,000 square feet, seven restaurants.

Siena— On the banks of the Truckee River, Tuscan village atmosphere, wine cellar.

Sundowner— Rustic two-floor casino downtown near Auto Museum and National Bowling Center.

Sands Regency— 800 slots, 10X craps odds, live entertainment nightly.

Peppermill— Located on South Virginia Ave, voted one of the top ten casinos in the U.S. by MSN.

Atlantis— Located on South Virginia Ave across from convention center. Seven restaurants, 24/7 gaming. One of three best poker rooms in U.S.

Sparks, Nevada

Six casinos are located in Sparks, a suburb that is known as Reno's sister city. Located one mile east on I-80, the casino district and the festival marketplace called Victorian Square have a turn-of-the-century theme. The square hosts special events throughout the year including summer concerts and the annual Victorian Christmas parade. Casinos in Sparks include:

Alamo Travel Center, 1959 East Greg Street
Baldini's Sports Casino, 865 South Rock Boulevard
John Ascuaga's Nugget, 1100 Nugget Avenue (the largest casino in Sparks)
Rail City Casino, 2121 Victorian Avenue
Silver Club Hotel/Casino, 1040 Victorian Avenue
Western Village Inn & Casino, 815 Nicholas Boulevard

Discounts at Sparks casinos include: discounts on food at Baldini's for seniors; 20% off the buffet at Rail City for seniors 50 and over; 10% off food at Silver Club for seniors 55 and older.

RV Resorts In Verdi

Two RV resorts at casinos are located in Verdi, four miles west of Reno (on I-80 at the California border): Boomtown and Gold Ranch.

Boomtown Hotel, Casino & RV Park
I-80 at Exit 4
Verdi, Nevada 89439 — **Map Location #5**
775-345-6000 • 800-648-3790
877-626-6686 (RV park)
www.boomtownreno.com

Description: The resort in the rolling hills of the Sierras, has a 338-room/suite hotcl and an RV park with 203 scenic full hookup sites. The RV park has an outdoor pool, two spas, family fun center with rides and arcade games, miniature golf, 24-hour mini-mart and free popcorn and coffee. Last year's rates were $22–$40. The casino features over 1,300 slots and 37 table games including #1 rated blackjack. A free shuttle runs to/from Reno.

Directions: From I-80 exit 4 (Boomtown/Garson Rd) north for .25 mile to the resort.

Gold Ranch Casino & RV Resort
I-80 at Exit 2
Verdi, Nevada 89439 — **Map Location #5**
775-345-6789 • 877-912-6789 (RV Resort)
www.goldranchrvcasino.com

Description: The modern resort has 105 paved, full hookup RV sites in the scenic Sierra Nevada locale that straddles the CA/NV border.

Amenities include heated pool/spa, horseshoes, laundry, showers and a 24-hour general store. 2005 daily RV rates were $24 –$27. A casino and full service travel center are in walking distance. The casino features 260 slots and a sports book (no table games) and the Sierra Café.

Directions: From I-80 exit 2 (Gold Ranch Rd) on the north side of the interstate.

Carson City Area

Carson City, named for adventurer Kit Carson, is Nevada's capital city. The city lies in a beautiful valley at the foot of the Sierras. Among the attractions is the Nevada State Museum, located in the building that once housed the Carson Mint, that made over $50 million in silver and gold coins until 1893. It is considered one of the West's top museums. Carson City is also home to the State Railroad Museum, the restored Old Capitol Building and Stewart Indian Museum.

Carson Nugget
507 North Carson Street
Carson City, Nevada 89701 — **Map Location #6**
775-882-1626 • 800-426-5239
www.ccnugget.com

Description: The casino, in the heart of Carson City, bills itself as the "Happiest Casino In The World." It features a rare collection of natural gold formations. The collection, which took 70 years to accumulate, includes leaf gold, wire gold, thread gold and crystallized gold just as they are found in nature. Its estimated value is over $1 million. The casino has 700 slot and video poker machines in denominations from pennies up, and pit/gaming tables. Restaurants include the buffet, a steakhouse, oyster bar and 24-hour coffee shop. The casino also has a motel and conference center.

Discounts: Seniors, 50 and older, receive 10% off food.

Directions & Parking: From Hwy-395 south exit 57B (Carson City & Virginia City), continue on Hwy-395 to Carson City. In Carson City, Hwy-395 is the same as Carson Street. The RV parking lot is at Stuart and Robinson, across the street from the back of the Nugget. The parking spots are back-ins and will fit RVs no longer than 38-foot. There are no hookups and the stay limit is 72 hours.

Piñon Plaza Casino Resort & RV Park
2171 Highway 50 East
Carson City, Nevada 89701 — **Map Location #6**
775-885-9000 • 877-519-5567
www.pinonplaza.com

Description: The RV park has 48 paved full hookup sites, laundry, horseshoes and modem hookup. The Best Western hotel has 148 rooms and RV guests are invited to use the pool/spa at the hotel. Daily RV rates in 2005 were from $22. The 24-hour casino has 328 slots, eight pit/table games, sports book and a 32-lane bowling alley. Restaurants include the Branding Iron Café and a steakhouse.

Discounts: Senior citizens, 55 and older, receive 10% off food. Good Sam and AAA discounts are honored.

Directions: From Jct. US-395 (Carson St). and US-50E (center of town), east one mile on US-50E. Boondocking is not permitted. RVs planning to stay overnight should pull into the RV park.

Carson Valley Inn & RV Park
1627 Highway 395 North
Minden, Nevada 89423 — **Map Location #6**
775-782-9711 • 800-321-6983
www.cvinn.com

Description: The resort is situated in a valley at the foot of the mountains surrounding Lake Tahoe. It includes a hotel, lodge and RV park. The RV park has 60 full hookup sites, pool/spa, CATV, game room and laundry.

There is a 14-day maximum stay. Last year's RV rates were from $22. The 20,000 square foot casino has slots, pit/table games and three restaurants (one is open 24 hours).

Discounts: Membership in the Senior Inn Club will get seniors 50 and older various discounts. RV guests receive a valuable fun book at check-in.

Directions: From Jct. US-395 & SR-88, south one mile on US-395.

Western Nevada (on US-95)

El Capitan Resort Casino
540 F Street (on US-95)
Hawthorne, Nevada 89415 — **Map location #7**
775-945-3321 • 800-922-2311
www.elcapitanresortcasino.com

Description: There is a 103-room hotel, a 10,000 square-foot casino and a restaurant at the site.

Discounts: Ask at the front desk about Fun Books.

Directions & Parking: The casino is on the northbound side of US-95. Free RV parking is on the east side of the casino building. Free overnight parking and a free RV dump are available, but there are no electric hookups.

Tonopah Station & RV Spaces
1137 Main Street
Tonopah, Nevada 89049 — **Map Location #8**
775-482-9777

Description: There are 20 full hookup spaces located behind the 103-room Ramada Hotel. Last year's RV rate was from $17. Pull into a site, then register at the hotel. There is a laundry room at the hotel. The sites are walking distance to the casino. The small Old West style casino, open 24 hours, has 90 slots in all denominations and a 24-hour restaurant and bar.

Directions: Located directly on US-95 at the south end of Tonopah.

Death Valley Region - near the CA/NV Border

Burro Inn Motel, Casino & RV Park
Highway 95 South & Third Street
Beatty, Nevada 89003 — **Map Location #9**
775-553-2225 • 800-843-2078
www.burroinn.com

Description: The RV park has 43 full hookup shaded mountain-view sites. Last year's RV rate was $15. The hotel has 62 rooms. There are 15 horseshoe pits at the resort. State horseshoe tournaments are held twice a year at the Burro Inn. Guests at the RV park get free passes to the town pool near the resort. The 24-hour casino has 62 slots and a gaming table plus a restaurant and bar.

Directions: Burro Inn is located on US-95 at the southern end of Beatty.

Longstreet Inn, Casino & RV Park
Route 373 HCR 70
Armagosa Valley, Nevada 89020 — **Map Location #10**
775-372-1777 • 800-508-9493
www.longstreetinn.com

Description: Located seven miles north of Death Valley, the RV park has 51 full hookup gravel sites, heated pool/spa, laundry and a 24-hour convenience store. Last year's RV rate was $16. The resort also has a 9-hole, par 3 golf course. The casino features 21 gaming tables, slots and video poker (no craps or roulette) and two restaurants.

Discounts: Seniors, 65 and older, receive 20% off food.

Directions: From Jct. US-95 & SR-373, southwest for 16 miles on SR-373 to CA/NV border.

Saddle West Casino & RV Park
1220 South Highway 160
Pahrump, Nevada 89048 — **Map Location #11**
775-727-1111 • 800-433-3987
www.saddlewest.com

Description: There is an RV park and a 157-room hotel at Saddle West. The RV park has 80 full service hookups, laundromat, pool/spa and gift shop. Last year's RV rates were from $18. Weekly and monthly rates are also available. The 19,000 square-foot casino features Nevada-style slots, video poker and table games and the Silver Spur restaurant. It is the closest RV park/casino to Death Valley National Park.

Discounts: Good Sam and Escapee discounts are honored at the RV park. There is a special senior citizen menu at the restaurant.

Directions: From Jct. of SR-160 & SR-372, south on SR-160 for .5 mile.

Terrible's Lakeside Casino & RV Park
5870 South Homestead Road
Pahrump, Nevada 89048 — **Map Location #11**
775-751-7770 • 888-558-LAKE
www.terribleherbst.com

Description: The RV park has 160 sites on a seven-acre lake offering fishing, swimming, peddle boats, kayaks, pool/spa, laundry and a 24-hour general store. Last year's rates were $22–$30. Weekly and monthly rates are also available. The 8,300 square-foot casino offers slots, video poker (no table games) and bingo every day in winter (five days in summer) plus a restaurant with buffet and menu service.

Discounts: Good Sam, AAA, AARP and FMCA discounts are honored at the RV park. Seniors, 55 and older, receive 10% off buffets.

Directions: From Jct. SR-160 & SR-372, go six miles south on SR-160, then 3.25 miles south on Homestead Road for 3.5 miles.

Indian Springs Casino & RV Park
372 Tonopah Highway (US-95)
Indian Springs, Nevada 89018 — **Map Location #12**
702-879-3456 • 877-977-7746
702-879-3129 (RV park)
www.indianspringscasino.com

Description: The 59 space RV park features full hookups at shaded sites, a convenience store and laundry. It is walking distance to the casino. Last year's rate was $16. The casino has 48 slots, blackjack tables, a 24-hour restaurant, lounge, video arcade and live music. There is a 45-room hotel on site.

Directions: Indian Springs is 35 miles northwest of Las Vegas; the casino is on Frontage Rd.

Northern Nevada Along I-80

West Wendover

The Montego Bay Casino and RV Park actually straddle the Nevada/Utah border along Interstate 80 in Wendover, UT and West Wendover, NV, with the RV park located in Utah but within walking distance to the casino in Nevada.

Montego Bay Casino and RV Park
100 Wendover Boulevard
West Wendover, Nevada 89883 — **Map Location #13**
775-664-9100

775-664-2221 or 800-848-7300 (RV park)
www.montegobaywendover.com

Description: The 56-space park has paved sites with full hookups, patios, grills, heated pool & spa, pavilion, horseshoes, game room and laundry. Last year's rate was $17. The casino complex includes 25,000 square feet of gaming plus eight restaurants. The casino is connected by a skyway to the State Line Nugget Casino on the other side of Wendover Blvd.

Discounts: Good Sam discount is honored at the RV park.

Directions: From I-80 Utah exit 2, go west for two miles on Wendover Blvd to First Street, then south for 200 feet.

State Line Nugget Casino
101 Wendover Boulevard
West Wendover, Nevada 89883 — **Map Location #13**
775-664-2221 • 800-648-9668
www.statelinenugget.com

Description: The 47,000 square-foot casino is connected by a sky bridge to Montego Bay Casino and RV Park. It has Vegas-style gaming and a 24-hour restaurant.

Peppermill Inn & Casino
680 Wendover Boulevard
West Wendover, Nevada 89883 — **Map Location #13**
775-664-2255 • 800-648-9660
www.peppermillwendover.com

Description: The 24,000 square foot casino has slots, table games and a 24-hour restaurant.

Directions & Parking: From I-80 exit 410, the casino is visible from the interstate. RVs should park in the lot on the east side of the hotel. Overnight is OK.

Rainbow Hotel Casino
1045 Wendover Boulevard
West Wendover, Nevada 89883 — **Map Location #13**
775-664-4000 • 800-217-0049
www.rainbowwendover.com

Description: The 47,500 square foot casino features hundreds of slots, 21 gaming tables, a poker room and two restaurants (buffets featured on weekends).

Discounts: Seniors, 65 and older, receive $2 off the buffet.

Directions & Parking: From I-80 exit 410, turn left at the stop sign and right on to Wendover Blvd. A parking lot for large vehicles is directly across the street from the casino. Overnight is permitted.

Wells

Two small casinos are located at I-80 exit 352 (Jct. US-93). They are:

Four Way Bar/Café & Casino (775-752-3344), 4,500 square feet of gaming with a restaurant,
Lucky J's Casino (775-752-2252), in the Flying J, 900 square feet of gaming and a restaurant.

Elko

Four casinos are located in Elko, and one – Gold Country Motor Inn – has a full service RV park. Elko is known as the home of Cowboy Poetry and the Mining Exposition.

Gold Country Motor Inn & RV Park
2050 Idaho Street
Elko, Nevada 89801 — **Map Location #15**
775-738-8421 • 800-621-1332

Description: The RV park has 26 back-in, full-hookup sites. CATV and phones are at each site. Last year's RV rates were from $20 and major discounts are accepted. RV guests should register at the Best Western front desk. The hotel has 140 rooms. The casino has 165 slots, three gaming tables, a restaurant and lounge. Gold Country is affiliated with Red Lion, Elko's largest casino located just across the street. Both are open 24 hours.

Directions: From I-80 exit 303 (east Elko), Gold Country is visible from the interstate.

Red Lion Inn & Casino
2065 Idaho Street
Elko, Nevada 89801 — **Map Location #15**
775-738-2111 • 800-545-0044
www.redlioncasino.com

Description: The 20,350 square foot casino in downtown Elko has over 500 slots, 21 gaming tables and two restaurants (one open 24 hours). The hotel has 223 rooms.

Directions & Parking: From I-80 exit 303, Red Lion is visible from the interstate and an RV park is located just across the street at Gold Country Motor Inn.

Commercial Casino
345 4th Street
Elko, Nevada 89801 — **Map Location #15**
775-738-3181 • 800-648-2345
www.fh-inc.com

Description: Over 100 years old, Commercial is the oldest continually operating casino in Nevada. A large gunfighter art collection is on display there. The casino has 243 slots and six gaming tables.

Directions & Parking: From I-80 exit 301, turn right into downtown.

RVs should use the lot at Stockman's Hotel & Casino, across the street; boondocking is OK.

Stockman's Hotel & Casino
340 Commercial Street
Elko, Nevada 89801 — **Map Location #15**
775-738-5141 • 800-648-2345
www.fh-inc.com

Description: An Old West themed casino, Stockman's has 217 slots and ten table games. The hotel has 141 rooms. It is across the street from the Commercial Casino.

Directions & Parking: From I-80 exit 301, turn right into the downtown area. The area for RV parking is across from the rear east corner of Stockman's.

Winnemucca

Model T Hotel, Casino & RV Park
1130 West Winnemucca Boulevard
Winnemucca, Nevada 89446 — **Map Location #16**
775-623-2588 • 800-645-5658
www.modelt.com

Description: The RV park has 58 level, paved pull-thru sites with full hookup, swimming pool, game room and laundry. Last year's RV rates were from $22. Shuttle service is provided to the casino. The casino features 24 hours of Nevada-style gaming including penny games, slots, table games and live keno plus a food court and country store. Live entertainment is featured on weekends. There is a 75-room hotel on site.

Discounts: FMCA discount is honored and a Fun Book with valuable casino coupons is given to all RV guests.

Directions: From I-80 exit 176, go .5 mile east on Winnemucca Blvd.

Note: The Red Lion Casino and Winners Casino are also located on West Winnemucca Blvd.

Jackpot

Jackpot, Nevada, a town of 1,500 residents, was the second casino boomtown after Las Vegas. Surrounded by mountain wilderness, Jackpot is a bright cluster of casinos located just south of the Idaho state line. There are also many outdoor recreational activities in and around Jackpot including excellent fishing in the nearby Little Salmon River and its tributaries.

Directions to Jackpot: From I-84 exit 173 in Idaho, go 42 miles south on US-93 —or— From I-80 exit 352 in Nevada go 68 miles north on US-93.

Cactus Pete's Resort Casino & RV Park
1385 Highway 93
Jackpot, Nevada 89825 — **Map Location #17**
775-755-2321 • 800-821-1103
www.ameristarcasinos.com

Description: The resort features a 91-space RV park, open year round, and a 302-room/suite hotel. RV guests are invited to use the amenities at the hotel. Last year's RV rates were $14 in season and $10 during winter months (No water in winter). There are five restaurants and a 26,000 square-foot casino at the resort. Headline entertainment is featured weekends in the Gala Showroom. The resort also has an 18-hole golf course.

Discounts: Seniors 60 and older receive discounts at the restaurant and gift shop. Free dinner is given to birthday celebrants. Dinner specials featured on Wednesdays.

Barton's Club 93
Highway 93
Jackpot, Nevada 89825 — **Map Location #17**
775-755-2341 • 800-258-2937

Description: This friendly 9,500 square-foot casino has slots and 13 gaming tables, There is a 104-room/suite hotel. Food venues include the Pair-A-Dice Buffet and a 24 hour full-service restaurant.

Discounts: Ask about the Fun Book.

Parking: Free overnight parking is permitted in the lot.

Horseshu Hotel and Casino
Highway 93
Jackpot, Nevada 89825 — **Map Location #17**
775-755-7777
www.ameristarcasinos.com

Description: Located directly across from Cactus Pete's, the resort has a 120 room/suite hotel and a casino with 124 slots and ten gaming tables. The Frontier Kitchen, open morning to night, specializes in Mexican favorites. Dancing to live Western bands is featured Wednesday through Sunday in the lounge.

Parking: Check in with Security for overnight parking in the lot.

New Jersey

In 1977 when the voters in New Jersey approved casino gambling, the state became the second in the U.S. to legalize gambling. The legislation was designed to revitalize Atlantic City, formerly the Queen of Resorts at the Jersey Shore.

The glitzy gaming industry restored part of Atlantic City's luster, but overall progress in reshaping the city has been slow. For gaming enthusiasts who travel by RV, there's good news and bad news. The good news: the trip to Atlantic City allows you to see the nation's only seaside casinos and experience the world-famous boardwalk. The bad news: your RV stay will be short because a city ordinance prohibits overnight parking.

Casinos along the boardwalk include: Atlantic City Hilton, Bally's, Caesars, Resorts, Sands, Showboat, Tropicana, Trump Plaza and Trump Taj Mahal. Marina casinos include: Borgata, Harrah's and Trump Marina. Casino to casino bus service is available.

Directions: Exit 38 from the Garden State Parkway to the Atlantic City Expressway that leads directly to the casino areas. Nine casinos are located along the Boardwalk at the ocean and three are in the marina area.

Parking: Harrah's at the Marina has a parking lot designated for large vehicles. The Convention and Visitors Authority notes that the following Boardwalk casinos have lots: the Trump Taj Mahal at Virginia Ave, Showboat at Delaware Ave or the Hilton at Boston Ave.

New Mexico

Various Pueblo and Apache Indian tribes own and operate New Mexico's casinos. Most casinos are located in the north central part of the state – the Santa Fe and Albuquerque areas. The Apache casino in southern New Mexico is a popular resort destination.

Full-service RV parks can be found at Dancing Eagle Casino on I-40 west of Albuquerque and San Felipe Hollywood Casino on I-25 north of Albuquerque.

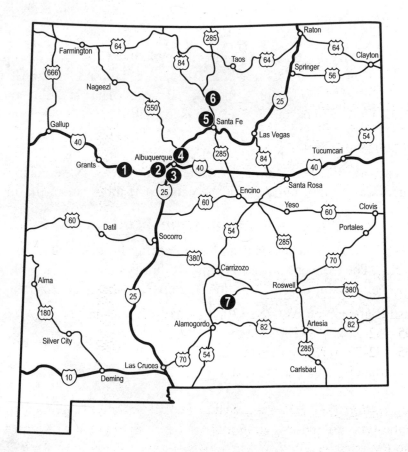

Albuquerque Area, page 187

Map	*Casino*
1	Dancing Eagle Casino & RV Park
1	Sky City Casino Hotel & Conference Center
2	Route 66 Casino
3	Isleta Casino & Resort
4	San Felipe Casino Hollywood & RV Park
4	Santa Ana Star Casino
4	Sandia Casino

Santa Fe Area, page 191

Map	*Casino*
5	Cities of Gold Casino Hotel
5	Camel Rock Casino
6	Big Rock Casino Bowl

Southern New Mexico, page 193

Map	*Casino*
7	Casino Apache / Inn of the Mountain Gods Resort

Albuquerque Area

Dancing Eagle Casino & RV Park
I-40 exit 108
Casa Blanca, New Mexico 87007 — **Map Location #1**
505-552-7777 • 877-440-9969
505-552-7730 (RV park)
www.dancingeaglecasino.com

Description: The RV park, casino and travel center are located in an adobe-type village owned and operated by the Pueblo of Laguna tribe. The RV park has 35 level gravel sites (some pull thrus) with water and electric, central dump, pet run, showers and laundry. The 2005 daily RV rate was $10. The travel center includes a supermarket, fast food, gas station, bakery and hair salon. The casino, walking distance from the RV park, features 500 slots (including over 100 penny machines) and ten tables plus a restaurant and gift shop. Casino hours are 8am–4am/24hrs (Thu–Sat).

Directions: From I-40 exit 108, the village is visible from the eastbound side of the interstate. RV parking is also permitted on any of the gravel areas adjacent to the paved casino parking lot.

Sky City Casino Hotel & Conference Center
I-40 exit 102
San Fidel, New Mexico 87049 — **Map Location #1**
505-552-6017 • 888-SKY-CITY
www.skycitycasino.com

Description: Owned and operated by the Acoma Pueblo, the 30,000 square-foot casino has 800 slots, ten gaming tables and a poker room. The Huwaka restaurant and buffet features Native, New Mexican and American cuisine. The Pinon Coffee Bar offers lighter fare. Hours are 8am–4am/24hrs (Thu–Sat). There is a 133-room hotel on site. The adjacent Sky City Travel Center is a popular stop for truckers. It has fuel services, a convenience store, laundromat and a small non-smoking slots-only casino.

Discounts: Seniors, 55 and older, get 10% off the buffet.

Directions & Parking: From I-40 exit 102, the casino can be seen from the westbound lanes. RVs should park east of the casino. Boondocking is permitted.

Route 66 Casino
I-40, exit 140
Albuquerque, New Mexico — **Map Location #2**
505-352-7866 • 866-352-7866
www.rt66casino.com

Description: The 50's-themed casino features 1,250 slots (with many progressives in all denominations), 20 pit/gaming tables, a 12-table poker room and bingo daily. Food venues include the Happy Cowboy Buffet and Johnny Rockets 50's style diner. Cabaret Dell Rhea features live entertainment on weekends. The Route 66 store has a wide variety of logo merchandise. Casino hours: 8am–4am/24hrs (Fri–Sat). An adjacent travel center caters to truckers and RVers and includes fuel services, a diner, convenience store, gift shop, snack bar and a slots-only casino.

Discounts: $1.99 late night specials at the restaurant.

Directions & Parking: The casino complex is visible from I-40 eastbound lanes at exit 140. RV parking areas are behind the casino building and at the travel center; overnight parking is permitted. Shuttle service is provided.

Isleta Casino & Resort
11000 Broadway S.E.
Albuquerque, New Mexico 87105 — **Map Location #3**
505-724-3800 • 877-7-ISLETA
www.isletacasinoresort.com

Description: The 100,000 square-foot casino has over 1,700 slots, 28 gaming tables, a poker room with six tables, five dining choices and a showroom with Vegas-style entertainment. Casino hours are 8am–4am/24hrs (Fri–Sat). The 27-hole Isleta Eagle golf course is just a chip shot away.

Discounts: Seniors, 55 and older, receive 13% off the buffet.

Directions & Parking: From I-25 exit 215, south on Hwy-47 for .5 mile. Parking for large vehicles is in the east lot (level gravel surface). Free overnight parking is permitted for RVs.

San Felipe Casino Hollywood & RV Park
25 Hagan Road

San Felipe Pueblo, New Mexico 87001 — **Map Location #4**
505-867-6700 • 877-529-2946
www.sanfelipecasino.com

Description: Next to I-25, the complex includes an RV park, travel
center and convenience store. The RV park has 50 sites with water and
electric and a central dump station. 2005 rates were $10 per night. RVers
should check in and pay at the casino before pulling in to a site. Security
will assist with parking. The casino has over 700 slots (including many
newly-released slots) and 15 tables, a buffet restaurant, high rollers grill
and gift shop. Casino hours are 8am–4am/24hrs (Fri–Sat). A 1,250-seat
amphitheater and the Hollywood Hills Raceway (Sprint Car Racing) are
located in the complex.

Discounts: New Players Club members receive matchplay.

Directions: I-25 at exit 252. The casino can be seen from northbound
side of the interstate. Overnight parking is permitted in the travel plaza
parking lot for RVs that do not want to use the hookups in the RV park.
All parking areas are walking distance to the casino.

Santa Ana Star Casino
54 Jemez Canyon Dam Road
Bernalillo, New Mexico 87004 — **Map Location #4**
505-867-0000
www.santaanastar.com

Description: The 19,000 square-foot Vegas-style casino has over 1,500
slots, 22 pit/gaming tables, eight-table poker room, four restaurants and
a 36-lane bowling alley. It is open 8am–4am/24 hrs (Fri–Sat).

Directions & Parking: From I-25 exit 242, west on Hwy-550 for two
miles. RV parking is in the lot west of the casino; shuttle service is
provided to the casino.

Sandia Casino

30 Rainbow Road
Albuquerque, New Mexico 87113 — **Map Location #4**
505-796-7500 • 800-526-9366
www.sandiacasino.com

Description: The large, modern casino with the majestic Sandia Mountains as a backdrop, has over 1,700 slots, 30 pit/gaming tables and the largest poker room in New Mexico. There is a separate non-smoking area and a high limits area. The resort includes a hotel, conference center and golf course. Restaurants include: Bien Shur for fine dining, a buffet restaurant and sandwich shop plus the Thiur Pa Lounge with nightly live entertainment. Casino hours are 8am–4am/24hrs (Thu–Sun).

Directions & Parking: From I-25 exit 234, east on Tramway Rd and turn left into the casino's main entrance. Designated RV parking is in the east parking lot near the hotel; it is walking distance to the casino. Overnight RV parking is permitted.

Santa Fe Area

Cities of Gold Casino Hotel

10-B Cities of Gold Road
Santa Fe, New Mexico 87506 — **Map Location #5**
505-455-3313 • 800-455-3313
www.citiesofgold.com

Description: The 40,000 square-foot casino features over 700 slots (lots of penny machines), 12 pit/gaming tables, a poker room with six tables and horse racing simulcasting, plus a buffet and snack bar. It is open 8am–4am/24hrs (Fri–Sun). The hotel on site has 124 rooms/suites. The Gold Dust Restaurant, located in the hotel, features Southwestern and American cuisine.

Discounts: Matchplay coupons are given to new Players Club members.

Directions & Parking: From I-25 exit 282-B (St. Francis Dr exit), north on Hwy-84/285 for 19 miles to Cities of Gold Rd exit. The casino is visible from the northbound side of the highway. RV parking is at the east end; follow signs for RV/truck parking. Overnight parking is permitted.

Camel Rock Casino
17486-A Highway 84/285
Santa Fe, New Mexico 87504 — **Map Location #5**
505-984-8414 • 800-GO-CAMEL
www.camelrockcasino.com

Description: The roomy Las Vegas-style casino with over 600 slots and ten pit/gaming tables is owned by the Pueblo of Tesuque. Casino hours: 8am–4am/24 hrs (Fri–Sat).

The nearby Flea Market (at exit 171, Flea Market Rd) with 400 booths is open Friday to Sunday, 8am–5pm, March thru November.

Discounts: A Fun Book with valuable coupons is given to new Players Club members. Senior discounts are offered for those 55 and older.

Directions: From I-25 exit 282-B, north on Hwy-84/285 for 13.6 miles to exit 175 (Camel Rock Rd). The casino is located next to the northbound side of 84/285. RV parking is in the large gravel lot north of the casino building. Overnight parking is permitted.

Big Rock Casino Bowl
419 North Riverside Drive
Espanola, New Mexico 87532 — **Map Location #6**
505-747-3100 • 866-244-7625
www.bigrockcasino.com

Description: This cozy casino is located in the heart of downtown Espanola, 25 miles north of Santa Fe. It has 400 slots, ten gaming tables and a bowling alley. Casino hours: 8am–4am/24hrs (Fri–Sat).

Discount: The restaurant features a $1.99 breakfast special.

Directions & Parking: From US-84/285 in Espanola, east on Fairview Dr (Rt-584) for 1.2 miles, south on Riverside Dr for one mile. Use the east end of the lot, next to the gas station. Overnight parking is allowed, but the parking lot is small and in a busy downtown area.

Southern New Mexico

Casino Apache / Inn of the Mountain Gods Resort
276 Carrizo Canyon Road
Mescalero, New Mexico 88340 — **Map Location #7**
505-464-4100 • 877-277-5677
www.innofthemountaingods.com/casino.htm

Description: The Mescalero Apache Tribe owns and operates two casinos on tribal land in rural southern New Mexico. A Travel Center casino is located convenient for travelers on Highway 70, one mile west of Ruidoso. With over 500 slots and ten gaming tables, the casino is open 24/7. There is also a convenience store, laundry and plenty of parking for large vehicles. Free shuttle service is provided to the larger casino at the Inn of the Mountain Gods, about four miles west of the travel center location.

The Inn of the Mountain Gods resort has a 275 room/suite hotel, four restaurants and a 50,000 square-foot casino with slots, pit/table games and a poker room.

Discounts: Seniors, 62 and older, get 20% off the buffet at the Inn. Tobacco products are sold at discounted prices in the smoke shop.

Directions & Parking: On Highway 70, the travel center has ample space for RV parking. Overnight parking is OK.

New York

Four Indian casinos are operating in upstate New York – three are listed here. A fourth Indian casino, in downtown Niagara Falls, does not have parking for large vehicles.

In 2001, legislation was passed to allow slot machines at the state's horse and harness race tracks, thus creating

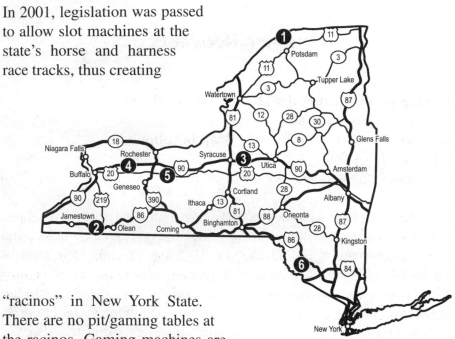

"racinos" in New York State. There are no pit/gaming tables at the racinos. Gaming machines are regulated by the New York State Lottery Division. New York State racinos are open from 10am–2am daily. Those listed here all permit free overnight parking for self-contained RVs. Race tracks not listed do not allow RV parking or are located in an area too congested for RVs.

Upstate New York, page 195

Map	Casino
1	Akwesasne Mohawk Casino
2	Seneca Allegany Casino
3	Turning Stone Casino Resort & RV Park

New York State Racinos, page 197

Upstate New York

Akwesasne Mohawk Casino
837 State Route 37
Hogansburg, New York 13655 — **Map Location #1**
518-358-2222 • 888-622-1155
www.mohawkcasino.com

Description: The casino has 1,000 slots and video poker machines available 24 hours and 25 pit/table games from 10am–4am. The poker room opens at 4pm weekdays, 11am weekends. Tournament action is featured Thursday through Sunday. The newly-renovated Native Harvest Buffet is open for breakfast, lunch and dinner, and the gift shop features Native American art.

Directions & Parking: From I-81 just north of Watertown, take Rt-37 north for about 65 miles to the casino, which is located just eight miles south of the US-Canada border in Hogansburg. After entering the casino property take the first driveway on the left to the large vehicle lot; 24-hour security is provided. Free overnight parking is permitted for self-contained RVs.

Seneca Allegany Casino
777 Seneca Allegany Boulevard
Salamanca, New York 14779 — **Map Location #2**
716-945-3200 • 877-553-9500
www.senecaalleganycasino.com

Description: The casino features 1,800 gaming machines and a full array of pit/gaming tables on a 122,000 square-foot gaming floor. There is a separate non-smoking casino and a poker room. Highlighting the food venues is Seneca's signature world-class Thunder Mountain Buffet. Snacks are served at Ricky's Café and Java Café.

Directions & Parking: The casino is located in Erie County, southwestern New York State, 65 miles south of Buffalo. From I-86 take exit 20. The casino can be seen on the south side of the interstate. There is ample parking lot space for large vehicles. Please check with Security if you plan to stay overnight.

Turning Stone Casino Resort & RV Park
5218 Patrick Road
Verona, New York 13478 — **Map Location #3**
315-361-7711 • 800-771-7711
www.turning-stone.com

Description: Owned by the Oneida Nation, the 100,000 square foot casino has cashless versions of traditional slots with PIN-controlled account cards that track the account balance, keno and lotto. Table games include blackjack, poker, craps, roulette, mini baccarat, sic bo and a poker room. The resort includes an RV park, inn, lodge and hotel, nine restaurants, three golf courses, an 800-seat showroom and a discount smoke shop.

The Villages at Turning Stone RV Park features 175 full-hookup, paved sites, including 50 pull thrus. The park has a heated pool and jacuzzi, nature trails and a wide variety of recreational activities including tennis, bocce ball, volleyball, basketball and horseshoes. The RV park is open April 22 through October 31. Shuttle service is provided to the casino.

Directions & Parking: The casino resort is located in central New York off I-90 directly at exit 33. Turn left from the exit, go to the stop light and turn left on to Rt-365. RVs should continue through the second light to the RV park.

New York State Racinos

Batavia Downs
8315 Park Road
Batavia, New York 14020 — **Map Location #4**
585-343-3750 • 800-724-2000
www.batavia-downs.com

Description: The oldest lighted harness track in the country features live harness racing Aug–Dec, Wed–Sat. The racino has over 100 slots and daily simulcasting of thoroughbred and harness racing. Dining options include Bijou Café for casual dining, Bijou Bar & Grille, for fine dining and The Buffet.

Directions & Parking: From I-90, exit 48, go through the toll booth and proceed straight through on to Veterans Memorial Drive for .2 mile. Turn left on to Park Rd for .3 mile to Batavia Downs. Check in with Security to verify where they want large vehicles to park.

Finger Lakes Gaming & Racetrack
5857 Route 96
Farmington, New York 14425 — **Map Location #5**
585-924-3232
www.fingerlakesracetrack.com

Description: This non-smoking racino features 28,000 square feet of gaming with over 1,000 slots and video poker machines. Live thoroughbred racing is held Fri–Tue from mid-April to late November. Simulcasting is offered every day. Food venues include Vineyard Food Court, Jake's Coffeehouse and the Sports Bar.

Directions & Parking: From NY State Thruway I-90, exit 44 take Rt-332 south for one mile to Rt-96, then left on Rt-96 for one-half mile. Check in with Security for parking directions.

Mighty M Gaming At Monticello Raceway
204 Route 17B
Monticello, New York 12701 — **Map Location #6**
845-794-4100 • 866-777-GAME
www.monticelloraceway.com

Description: The raceway features live harness racing year-round, Sun–
Wed. The racino has 1,800 slots in denominations from two cents to
$10. There is a high limits area. Daily simulcasting features thoroughbreds
and harness racing. Dining options include the Winners Circle Buffet
and a food court. Nightly entertainment is featured in the Lava Lounge.

Directions & Parking: The raceway is located directly on Rt-17B, 50
miles west of Newburgh. Please check with Security if you plan to park
overnight.

North Carolina

North Carolina is home to a single casino – Harrah's Cherokee Casino located in the Smokey Mountains in the western part of the state, some 55 miles west of Ashville. The facility is owned by the Eastern Band of Cherokee Indians.

Western North Carolina, page 199

Map	Casino
1	Harrah's Cherokee Casino

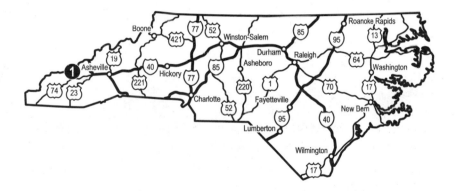

Western North Carolina

Harrah's Cherokee Casino
777 Casino Drive
Cherokee, North Carolina 28719 — **Map Location #1**
828-497-7777 • 800-HARRAHS
www.harrahs.com

Description: The casino features approximately 4,000 slots and video poker machines in denominations from nickels and up. There are 36 tables with digital games, live dealers and real chips on a video table. The casino floor also includes a high limits area and a separate non-smoking slots area. The luxury hotel has 596 rooms and a conference center. Food venues include the Fresh Market Buffet, a steakhouse in the casino and a café in the hotel.

Directions & Parking: From the Ashville, NC area, take I-40 exit 27, west on Hwy-74 to exit 74, then north on US-441 for approximately four miles into Cherokee, then right at the first light to the casino. From the Knoxville, TN area, take I-40 exit 407 to TN Hwy-66/US 441. Then south on US-441 into Cherokee and left at the third traffic light (Hwy-19 north) to the casino. RVs should park along the fence on the far west side of the main parking lot. Overnight parking is permitted.

North Dakota

North Dakota's casino resorts, located in several areas of the state, all have hotels and most have campgrounds or hookups available for RV travelers. Although the casinos and hotels are open all year, some campgrounds close during winter months. North Dakota, known as the state "Where The West Begins," offers scenic beauty, lots of outdoor non-gaming activities and a strong influence of Native American heritage. All North Dakota casinos are open 24 hours.

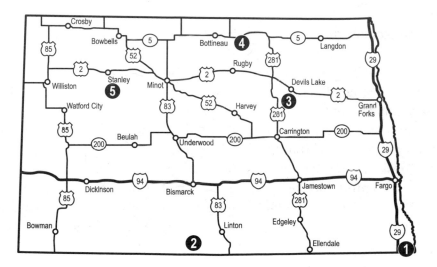

Southern North Dakota, page 202

Upstate North Dakota, page 203

Southern North Dakota

Dakota Magic Casino & RV Spaces
16849 102nd Street SE
Hankinson, North Dakota 58041 — **Map Location #1**
701-634-3000 • 800-325-6825
www.dakotamagic.com

Description: The casino complex, owned and operated by the Sisseton-Wahpeton Sioux Tribe, includes a hotel with 122 rooms/suites and an entertainment/conference center. 25 RV spaces with full hookups are on the north side of the casino (electric only during winter months). Last year's rate was $10.50 per night. RV guests should register at the hotel front desk. The casino has over 600 reel slot machines, 13 pit/gaming tables, a comfortable high limits area with slots and tables, poker room, live keno and a pari-mutuel betting parlor. Restaurants include The Buffet and Seven Fires with menu service. The Dakota Winds Golf Course is adjacent to the casino.

Discounts: A Fun Book is given to all hotel and RV guests. Ask about senior citizen discounts on Mondays. Stay and Play golf packages are also available from the hotel.

Directions: The casino is just off I-29 at exit 1 at the ND/SD state line.

Prairie Knights Casino Resort & RV Spaces
7932 Highway 24
Fort Yates, North Dakota 58538 — **Map Location #2**

701-854-7777 • 800-425-8277
www.prairieknights.com

Description: The resort is owned and operated by the Standing Rock Sioux Indian Community. There are 96 rooms/suites, conference and banquet rooms in the lodge and 12 RV (electric only) spaces within walking distance of the casino. Last year's daily rate for RV sites was $5. Pull into a site first, then register at the hotel desk. A 24-hour gas station and Quik Mart, bait and tackle shop and central dump are near the RV sites at the casino. The modern Vegas-style casino has 600 slots, nine gaming tables and a poker room. The Feast of the Rock Buffet is open morning to night and Hunter's Club fine dining is open for dinner Tuesday through Sunday. Headline entertainment is featured on weekends at the 2,350-seat pavilion. The Marina at Prairie Knights is a few miles down the hill from the casino/lodge. It has 32 sites with electric and fire rings at a daily rate of $10. A central dump and fresh water supply are available for campers at the marina. There is a boat ramp with access to the 231-mile long Lake Oahe reservoir on the Missouri River where anglers can hook walleye, northern pike, Chinook salmon, perch and bass. Shuttle service is provided between the marina and the casino. There is 24-hour security throughout the resort.

Discounts: Seniors, 55 and older, get a $6.75 buffet, 11am–5pm weekdays. Buffet specials are offered on concert days.

Directions: From I-94 at Manden (exit 152), go south on Sunset Dr for .8 mile; the street name changes to 6th Ave NW, go another .5 mile and turn left on Main St W through Manden, then south on 6th Ave SE (Hwy-1806) for 46 miles.

Upstate North Dakota

Spirit Lake Casino Resort & RV Spaces
7889 Highway 57
Spirit Lake, North Dakota 58370 — **Map Location #3**

701-766-4747 • 800-WIN-U-BET
www.spiritlakecasino.com

Description: Located on the scenic shores of Devil's Lake in the central region of the state, the resort has a 124-room hotel, RV sites and a marina. There are 15 RV sites with electric (open all year) around the back perimeter of the fully paved parking lot. Last year's daily rate was $18. RV guests are invited to use the hotel amenities that include a large indoor pool, whirlpool, water slide and fitness room. RV reservations are suggested during warm weather months. Boat rentals and fishing services are available at the marina. The 45,000 square foot casino has over 600 coinless slots, ten gaming tables, a poker room and three restaurants. It is open 24 hours.

Discounts: A Fun Book with dining, gaming and gift shop discount coupons is given to all RV and hotel guests. There is a discount smoke shop on the premises.

Directions: From I-29 exit 141, west on Hwy-2 for 86 miles to Devil's Lake, then south on Hwy-20 for five miles and continue on Hwy-57 for another 1.5 mile.

Sky Dancer Hotel & Casino
Highway 5 West
Belcourt, North Dakota 58316 — **Map Location #4**
701-244-2400 • 866-244-9467
www.skydancercasino.com

Description: The 24-hour casino has 500 slots (1¢ to $5), eight gaming tables, a poker room, simulcast racing and a restaurant/snack bar. There is a hotel with 140 rooms/suites, indoor pool and gift shop.

Directions & Parking: From I-29 exit 203, west on Hwy-81, then west on Hwy-5. The casino is five miles west of the town of Belcourt between MP 243 & 244 on Hwy-5. Adequate RV parking is available in the casino parking lot and overnight is OK. The casino is ten miles south of the Canada border.

Four Bears Casino & Lodge & RV Park
202 Frontage Road
New Town, North Dakota 58763 — **Map Location #5**
701-627-4018 • 800-294-5454
www.4bearscasino.com

Description: Located on the shores of Lake Sakakawee, the third largest man-made lake in the U.S. with 1,500 miles of shoreline, Four Bears is a popular fishing destination. The lodge has 97 rooms. There are 85 full-hookup RV spaces located about one-quarter mile behind the lodge/casino building. Most sites are occupied seasonally; it is advisable to call ahead to check on availability. Last year's daily rate was $12. The campground closes for the winter season. The casino has 500 slots, nine pit/gaming tables, poker room and a restaurant/snack bar.

Directions: Nearly 100 miles from the nearest interstate, the drive into Four Bears involves narrow two-lane roads and steep grades. From I-94 exit 61, go north on Hwy-22 for 83 miles, then east on Hwy-23 for 2.1 miles to the casino.

Oklahoma

Oklahoma has more Native American tribes than any other state. There are some 80 Indian gaming locations throughout Oklahoma. Because this book is designed for RVers on the road, we've included only the larger, 24-hour facilities that either have a campground or allow secure overnight parking for RVs. When traveling in Oklahoma, you might see many small buildings with a "casino" sign…some are even near an interstate. But, generally the smaller facilities are not open 24 hours and do not allow RV parking. Be sure to check with Security before parking at a casino not listed in this guide.

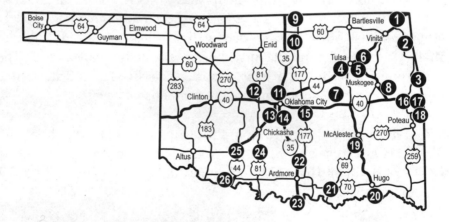

A major expansion in gaming took place after a statewide gaming referendum in November 2004 received voter approval. The expanded gambling allowed Indian casinos to add live table games, including blackjack and poker. Many of Oklahoma's Indian casinos now have poker rooms. The expansion of gambling also included video poker and faster slots at Indian casinos.

Oklahoma's three horse racing tracks also benefited from the 2004 referendum. Slots (but no table games) were approved for the state's race tracks and in 2005 all became "racinos." Remington Park in Oklahoma City added 650 machines; Blue Ribbon Downs in Sallisaw and Will Rogers Downs in Claremore each added 250 slots. The new "racinos" are listed along with the other casinos in their part of the state.

Northeastern Oklahoma, page 208

Map	*Casino*
1	Buffalo Run Casino
1	Quapaw Casino
1	The Stables Casino
2	Grand Lake Casino
3	Cherokee Casino – Siloam Springs
4	Osage Million Dollar Elm Casino
5	Cherokee Casino Resort
6	Cherokee Casino/Will Rogers Downs & RV Park
7	Creek Nation Casino – Okmulgee
8	Creek Nation Casino – Muskogee

North Central Oklahoma, page 213

Map	*Casino*
9	Kaw Nation Bingo & RV Spaces
10	7 Clans Paradise Casino & RV Spaces

Oklahoma City Area, page 214

Map	*Casino*
11	Remington Park Racino
12	Lucky Star Casino & RV Spaces – Concho
13	Newcastle Gaming Center
14	Thunderbird Wild Wild West Casino
15	Fire Lake Entertainment Center & Campground

Southeastern Oklahoma, page 217

Map	*Casino*
16	Blue Ribbon Downs Racino
17	Cherokee Casino – Roland
18	Choctaw Gaming Center – Pocola

19   Chocktaw Casino – McAlester
20   Choctaw Casino – Grant
21   Choctaw Casino – Durant

South Central Oklahoma, page 219

Map   *Casino*
22   Treasure Valley Casino
23   Win Star Casino
24   Marlow Gaming Center
25   Fort Sill Apache Casino
25   Comanche Nation Casino & RV Spaces
26   Comanche Red River Casino & RV Spaces

Northeastern Oklahoma

Buffalo Run Casino
1000 Buffalo Run Blvd
Miami, Oklahoma 74354 — **Map Location # 1**
www.buffalorun.com

Description: The casino, located near the Miami exit off I-44, features 750 slots in all denominations, a sports simulcasting area, ten-table poker room and 12 blackjack tables. The pretty Coleman Restaurant is open daily for lunch and dinner. There is a snack bar in the casino. Live entertainment is featured on weekends.

Directions & Parking: From I-44 exit 313 (Miami), after the toll booth, continue straight on US-69A for 1.5 mile. If playing at the casino, free overnight parking is available for RVs.

Quapaw Casino
US-69A
Miami, Oklahoma 74355 — **Map Location # 1**
877-569-1500
www.quapawcasino.net

Description: The pleasant, roomy casino has over 400 slots in all denominations, video poker, 15 blackjack tables ($2 minimums available) and a non-smoking poker room. Live entertainment is featured on weekends in the sports bar. There are several pull-thru RV spaces with water and electric and a central dump on the east side of the parking lot. Please sign in and register at the front desk of the casino to use an RV site. There is no charge for the first three days.

Directions & Parking: From I-44 exit 313, after going through the toll booth, continue straight on US-69A north for 3.5 miles and turn right into the casino.

The Stables Casino
530 H Street SE
Miami, Oklahoma 74354 — **Map Location # 1**
877-774-7884

Description: The casino has over 500 slots and video poker machines, electronic blackjack and three-card poker machines, and an off track betting parlor with national simulcast of top thoroughbred horse races. There is live action blackjack and a poker room on the second floor. The Clubhouse Restaurant serves Sunday brunch, 10–2, and lunch and dinner every Tuesday through Saturday.

Directions & Parking: From I-44 exit 313, after going through the toll booth turn left and go one mile west on SR-10, then left on H St, for two blocks. RV parking is on the south side of the parking lot and is available for those playing in the casino. Please check in with Security if you plan to stay overnight.

Grand Lake Casino
24701 South 655th Road
Grove, Oklahoma 74344 — **Map Location # 2**
918-786-8528 • 800-426-4640
www.grandlakevisitor.com

Description: Located 90 miles east of Tulsa near a popular fishing lake, the casino is open 24/7 and has 630 slots, live gaming tables, poker room and race book. Live bingo is held every day.

Directions & Parking: From I-44 exit 302 (Afton/Fairland) take Hwy-60 east through Fairland and past Twin Bridges State Park to Wyandotte. Continue to the junction of Hwy-10 south (the second Hwy-10 junction where there is a large casino sign). Go south on Hwy-10 for about 11 miles along the lake. The casino is on the right side. RVs should park on the north side of the lot. Check in with Security if you plan to stay overnight.

Note: Bordertown Casino, located on the Oklahoma/Missouri border in Seneca, MO, is listed in the Missouri section of this guide.

Cherokee Casino – Siloam Springs
7300 Highway US-412
West Siloam Springs, Oklahoma 74338 — **Map Location # 3**
918-422-6301 • 800-256-2338
www.cherokeecasino.com/siloam

Description: The casino, open 24/7 has over 800 slots, live blackjack, a poker room and bingo. There is a deli restaurant.

Directions & Parking: The casino is located directly at the junction of US-412 and Hwy-59 near the Arkansas border. RVs should park in the west lot. Overnight parking is permitted.

Osage Million Dollar Elm Casino
301 Blackjack Drive
Sand Springs, Oklahoma 74063 — **Map Location # 4**
877-246-8777
www.milliondollarelm.com

Description: The friendly 25,000 square-foot casino features 500 electronic gaming devices in all denominations, live action blackjack tables, food court, bar, lounge and live entertainment.

Directions & Parking: From I-44 exit 231, take US-64 west/SR-51 west toward Sand Springs for 15.5 miles to the 129th West Ave exit. At the end of the exit ramp, turn left, then turn right and go north up the long hill for 1.5 mile and turn left into the casino. RVs should park on the west side of the parking lot. Free overnight parking is permitted.

Cherokee Casino Resort
19105 East Timbercrest Circle
Catoosa, Oklahoma 74015 — **Map Location # 5**
918-384-7800 • 800-760-6700
www.cherokeecasino.com/catoosa

Description: The large casino resort includes a hotel and golf course. The 80,000 square-foot casino has 1,600 slots, 60 live blackjack and three-card poker tables and a 30-table poker room. Tournaments are held in the poker room as well as qualifying rounds for the World Poker Tour. Food venues include Wild Potato Buffet, McGill's Steakhouse, Sidewalk Café and Cabin Creek Smokehouse. There is live entertainment in the lounge.

Discounts: Ask about weekly Senior Day specials and Men's and Ladies nights.

Directions & Parking: From I-40 exit 240A (193rd East Ave) turn right, stay in the left lane and turn left at the light. Parking for RVs and motor coaches is north of the casino building. Please follow signs and check in with Security if you plan to stay overnight.

Cherokee Casino/Will Rogers Downs & RV Park
20900 South 4200 Road
Claremore, Oklahoma 74017 — **Map Location # 6**
918-283-8800
www.cherokeecasino.com

Description: In 2004, the Cherokee Nation purchased Will Rogers Downs. There is a full-service RV park at the facility. The "racino" has

250 electronic gaming machines, race simulcasting and a Bar & Grille. Thoroughbred racing takes place February through May. The RV park has 426 full hookup sites and is open year round.

Directions & Parking: The racino is located directly on Hwy-20 east of Claremore. From I-44 (Will Rogers Turnpike) take exit 255, then east on Hwy-20 for four miles. Check in with Security if you want to stay in the parking lot.

Creek Nation Casino – Okmulgee
1901 North Wood Drive
Okmulgee, Oklahoma 74447 — **Map Location # 7**
918-756-8400
www.creeknationcasino.com

Description: The small, friendly 10,000 square-foot casino features 385 slots, live action blackjack (with $2 minimums), poker room and daily bingo.

Discounts: Ask about weekly special promotions for seniors 50 and older.

Directions & Parking: From I-40 exit 240B, take US-75 north for 15 miles. (Note: rough pavement on sections of US-75). The casino is located at the intersection of US-75 and East Eufala St in North Okmulgee and can be accessed from the northbound lanes of US-75. Free RV parking is available along the back perimeter of the parking lot. Please check with Security if you plan to stay overnight.

Creek Nation Casino – Muskogee
3420 West Peak Boulevard
Muskogee, Oklahoma 74403 — **Map Location # 8**
918-683-1825
www.creeknationcasino.com

Description: The 22,500 square-foot casino has 600 electronic gaming machines, including video poker, live action blackjack, poker room and separate non-smoking gaming rooms. The café is open late. Complimentary non-alcoholic beverages are offered to all players. An adjacent travel plaza has a discount smoke shop.

Directions & Parking: From I-40 exit 264, go north on US-69 to Muskogee. Exit at Tahlequah and go to the stop sign, then west under US-69. The casino is on the right. Overnight RV parking is available; please check in with Security.

North Central Oklahoma

Kaw Nation Bingo & RV Spaces
5640 North LaCann Drive
Newkirk, Oklahoma 74647 — **Map Location # 9**
580-362-2578

Description: The casino has 450 slots, live action blackjack tables, poker room and The Eatery Restaurant.

Directions & Parking: From I-35 exit 222 take Hwy-11 east toward Blackwell for 15 miles to Hwy-77 north. North on Hwy-77 for six miles to Newkirk. Turn right at the traffic light and proceed for one mile, then turn right for about three blocks to the casino. RV spaces with free electric hookups are available.

7 Clans Paradise Casino & RV Spaces
7500 Highway 177
Red Rock, Oklahoma 74651 — **Map Location # 10**
580-723-4005 ·866-723-4005

Description: The 23,000 square-foot casino has over 500 slots, live action blackjack, poker room, OTB race book and two restaurants. It is open 10am–2am/24 hrs (Fri-Sat). There are seven RV spaces with electric and water hookups available. First day is free and there is a $7 per day charge thereafter.

Discounts: Thursday is Senior Day with free lunch offered 11:30am–1:30pm and $5 matchplay.

Directions & Parking: From I-35 exit 194 take US-412 east for about 12 miles to the Stillwater/Ponca City exit / US-177. Go north on US-177 for seven miles to the casino. RVs should register at the Players Club desk.

Oklahoma City Area

Remington Park Racino
One Remington Place
Oklahoma City, Oklahoma 73111 — **Map Location # 11**
405-424-1000 • 800-456-9000
www.remingtonpark.com

Description: The raceway has rejuvenated its second floor area into a slots-only casino featuring 650 electronic gaming machines, racebook, sports bar and a buffet restaurant. The racino is open Sun–Wed, 10am–midnight and Thu–Sat, 10am–3am. Live thoroughbred horse racing takes place Mon–Fri in season and there is daily simulcasting.

Directions & Parking: Remington is located at the junction of Interstates 35 and 44 in the heart of the Oklahoma City Adventure District. From I-35, exit at 50th and proceed to Gate 1. There is a separate bus parking lot. Please check in with Security if you plan to stay overnight.

Lucky Star Casino & RV Spaces – Concho
7777 North Highway 81
Concho, Oklahoma 73022 — **Map Location # 12**
405-262-7612
www.luckystarcasino.org

Description: The 40,000 square-foot casino is open 24/7. There are 750 slots, blackjack tables and a poker room. The Concho Café serves American-style breakfast, lunch and dinner daily. There is a separate smoke shop on the property.

Directions & Parking: From I-40 exit 125, take US-81 north for eight miles to the casino. The casino complex is located on the southbound side of US-81. RV spaces with electric, water and sewer hookups are located on the east side of the casino building. Please sign in and register at the security desk in the casino before hooking up. There is no charge for the spaces.

Newcastle Gaming Center
2457 Highway 62 Service Road
Newcastle, Oklahoma 73065 — **Map Location # 13**
405-387-6013
www.chickasaw.net

Description: Located south of Oklahoma City, the 24-hour casino in two buildings features 900 slots, off track betting, 14 blackjack tables ($3 minimums) and a poker room. Blackjack tables are open 24 hours. Kentucky Fried Chicken fast food is located on the premises and there is a restaurant in the casino. A smoke shop is also located in the casino.

Discounts: Senior citizen day every Wednesday with free coffee and donuts 9–11am.

Directions & Parking: From I-44 Newcastle exit 107, follow US-62 west. Cross the bridge that curves back over the interstate. Near the end of the bridge, slow down and be prepared to make the first left turn, crossing over the eastbound lanes of US-62 into the casino driveway; then make an immediate left and drive to the large gravel parking lot on the north side of the complex. Park parallel to the grassy area; free overnight parking is permitted.

Thunderbird Wild Wild West Casino
15100 East Highway 9
Norman, Oklahoma 73026 — **Map Location # 14**
405-360-9270 • 800-259-LUCK
www.shawneecasinos.com

Description: The western-themed Vegas-style casino features 1,200 electronic gaming machines, blackjack tables, poker room and the Boots & Saddles Restaurant. The casino is open 24/7.

Directions & Parking: From I-35 exit 108, take Hwy-9 east toward Tecumsah for 17.5 miles. RV parking spaces are behind the casino building and overnight is OK.

Fire Lake Entertainment Center & Potawatomi Campground
1601 South Gordon Cooper Drive
Shawnee, Oklahoma 74801 — **Map Location # 15**
405-273-2242 • 405-878-4664
www.potawatomi.org

Description: The 24/7 casino features 700 slots, live action at 11 blackjack tables with $2 minimums, poker room, off track betting, bingo and a separate non-smoking area. There is The Bistro buffet restaurant and two full-service bars. Complimentary ice cream and soft drinks are available for players.

The Potawatomi Campground is about a block away from the casino building, located on the south side of the Fire Lake Discount Food Store (which is between the casino and the campground). Last year's per night charge was $11 for electric and water hookups. Campground registration is at the Tribal Administration Building (on the east side of Gordon Cooper Blvd) 9am–5pm on weekdays or at the Police Station in front of the casino building, evenings and weekends.

Directions & Parking: From I-40 exit 181 (Shawnee) go south on Hwy-177 for seven miles. Then turn left on Hardesty Rd (blinking light at the corner) then east for about one mile to Gordon Cooper Dr. Turn right on

Gordon Cooper and turn right at the second driveway into the strip mall lot. (Note: Be sure to use the second driveway (close to the casino building)). The third driveway (in front of the food market) has a sharp dip and can cause a rig to bottom-out. Free overnight parking is available near the casino. If going into the campground, enter from Gordon Cooper Dr and cross the lot at the front of the strip mall to the campground entrance on the south side of the parking area. Do not go into the campground from the road that runs on the west side, (behind the casino/strip mall/campground complex) because there is a deep gully on that side of the campground.

Southeastern Oklahoma

Blue Ribbon Downs Racino
3700 West Cherokee Street
Sallisaw, Oklahoma 74955 — **Map Location # 16**
918-775-7771
www.blueribbondowns.net

Description: Blue Ribbon Downs is Oklahoma's oldest racing facility and its first pari-mutuel race track. It opened in 1962 and began pari-mutuel racing in 1984. Owned and operated by the Choctaw Nation, the racino has 250 slots and a snack bar. Live racing of thoroughbreds, quarter horses, paint and appaloosas in held in season (May–Sept) and there is daily simulcasting.

Directions & Parking: Blue Ribbon Downs is located off I-40 at exit 308. From exit 308 take Hwy-52 north to the second stop light, then go west on Hwy-64 for about three miles to Blue Ribbon on the south side of the highway. There is ample parking for large vehicles, but check-in with Security is required if you want to stay overnight.

Cherokee Casino – Roland
I-40 and Hwy-64 at Exit 325
Roland, Oklahoma 74954 — **Map Location # 17**
918-427-7491 • 800-256 2338
www.cherokeecasino.com/roland

Description: The casino has over 500 slots, live blackjack tables, a poker room and a 600-seat bingo hall. The sidewalk café features a deli menu.

Directions & Parking: The casino is on the north side of I-40 at exit 325. RVs should use the large lot behind the casino building. (Note: Go all the way to the end of the Days Inn lot before turning into the casino lot.) Overnight parking is permitted for self-contained RVs.

Choctaw Gaming Center – Pocola
3400 Choctaw Road
Pocola, Oklahoma 74902 — **Map Location # 18**
918-436-7761 • 800-590-5825
www.choctawcasinos.com

Description: The casino has 1,000 slots, a 100-seat OTB area, a 300-seat bingo pavilion and showroom and live blackjack. There is a buffet restaurant and a 24-hour snack bar.

Directions & Parking: From I-40 in Arkansas, take exit 7 (Ft. Smith/ Van Buren) to I-540 south to the Arkoma exit. The casino is visible from I-540. RV parking is available at the back of the casino building; overnight is OK.

Choctaw Casino – McAlester
1638 South George Nigh Expressway
McAlester, Oklahoma 74501 — **Map Location # 19**
918-423-8161 • 877-904-8444
www.choctawcasinos.com

Description: The 17,500 square-foot casino is open 24/7. It features slots and video poker machines. There is live simulcast horse racing of the most popular tracks seven days a week. An adjacent travel plaza also has electronic gaming machines, discount smoke shop, snacks, gas and parking for large vehicles.

Directions & Parking: From I-40 in the Checotah area (milepost 264), go south on US-69 through McAlester. The casino is located five miles south of McAlester on the northbound side of the highway. RVs should use the truck parking lot; Security will assist with parking.

Choctaw Casino – Grant
Route 1
Grant, Oklahoma 74738 — **Map Location # 20**
580-326-8397
www.choctawcasinos.com

Description: Located on Hwy-271 north of Paris, Texas, the casino has 625 slots, blackjack tables and a deli.

Parking: RVs should park in the lot north of the casino building; overnight is OK.

Choctaw Casino – Durant
3735 Choctaw Road, Highway 69/75
Durant, Oklahoma 74701 — **Map Location # 21**
580-920-0160 • 800-788-2464
www.choctawcasinos.com

Description: The 36,000 square-foot casino has over 800 slots, blackjack tables, OTB, a 750-seat bingo hall and the Three Arrows Buffet. Simulcast horse racing features the most popular tracks. The 42-room Choctaw Inn is on site. There are two adjacent travel plazas with smoke shops. The casino is open 24/7.

Directions: The casino is located just north of the Texas state line on the northbound side of Hwy-69/75. Security will assist with RV parking.

South Central Oklahoma

Treasure Valley Casino
I-35 Exit 55
Davis, Oklahoma 73030 — **Map Location # 22**

580-369-2895
www.chicasaw.net

Description: The casino has 300 electronic gaming machines, live action blackjack tables, buffet restaurant and snack bar. The casino is open 24/7; hours for blackjack are 11am–3am. OTB is available and there is a Microtel motel on site.

Directions & Parking: From I-35 exit 55, follow signs to the casino. Free RV parking is available on the east side of the casino building. Please notify Security if you plan to stay overnight.

Win Star Casino
I-35 Exit 1
Thackerville, Oklahoma 73459 — **Map Location # 23**
580-276-4229 ·800-622-6317

Description: There are three casinos on a 110,000 square-foot gaming floor: Center Ring, circus-themed, Palace-themed and Mariachi, Latin fiesta-themed all open 8am–6am daily. The Vegas-style gaming features 2,100 coinless slots, OTB betting center, poker room (noon–3am) and blackjack tables (10am–3am). Food venues include: Zar's Italian Kitchen, Stone Ranch Steakhouse, Bread Basket Buffet and Midway fast food area. There is a 1,200-seat showplace theater featuring headline entertainment. The Thackerville Travel Plaza with gas, 96 slots and fast food is nearby.

Discounts: Ask about free breakfast for seniors 55+ on Senior Day.

Directions & Parking: Located on I-35 at exit 1, one mile north of the Red River TX/OK border. RVs should park at the south side of the lot. Please check in with Security if you plan to stay overnight.

Marlow Gaming Center
Route 3
Marlow, Oklahoma 73055 — **Map Location # 24**
580-255-1668
www.chicasaw.net

Description: The casino has 380 slots and a buffet restaurant. It is open daily 9am–7am. RV spaces with hookups are being planned for the future.

Directions: From I-44, take the second Chickasha exit to US-81 south. Stay on US-81 south through the town of Marlow and past the Y in the road. RVs should park on the south side of the casino building, near the Lighthorse Police Department building.

Fort Sill Apache Casino
2315 East Gore Boulevard
Lawton, Oklahoma 73502 — **Map Location # 25**
580-248-5905

Description: The 7,700-square foot casino has slots only and is open 24/7. There is a snack bar in the casino.

Directions & Parking: From I-44 exit 37 go east on Gore Blvd for about one-quarter mile. The casino is on the south side of Gore Blvd. RVs should park in the gravel parking area west of the casino building; overnight is OK.

Comanche Nation Casino & RV Spaces
402 South Interstate Drive
Lawton, OK 73502 — **Map Location # 25**
580-354-2000 • 866-354-2500
www.comanchenationgames.com

Description: Open 24/7, the casino features 480 slots, live action blackjack and poker, off track betting, bingo and a restaurant and snack bar. The casino offers free electric hookups for RVs.

Directions & Parking: From I-44 exit 37 (Gore Blvd), the casino can be seen from the eastbound lanes of the interstate. RV spaces with electric hookups are located behind the bingo hall. Check in with Security if you plan to stay overnight.

Comanche Red River Casino & RV Spaces
Highway 36 and Highway 70
Devol, Oklahoma 73531 — **Map Location # 26**
580-299-3378 • 866-280-3261

Description: The casino features over 1,000 slots, blackjack tables, poker room and a restaurant. The casino offers free electric hookups for RVs.

Directions & Parking: From I-44 exit 4, take US-70 west for about seven miles to the casino. Electric hookup RV spaces are at the south side of the parking lot. Register at the front desk.

Oregon

The seven Indian casinos in Oregon listed here are located within an easy drive of an interstate or major highway. Most rank among the top Oregon attractions according to the State's Department of Tourism. Spirit Mountain Casino is the number one Oregon destination.

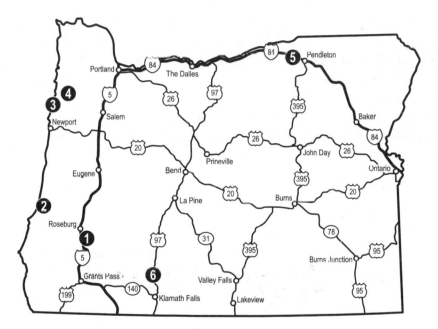

Western Oregon, page 224

Eastern Oregon (off I-84), page 226

Map   Casino
5   Wildhorse Resort & Casino & RV Park

Western Oregon

Seven Feathers Hotel & Casino Resort & RV Park
146 Chief Miwaleta Lane
Canyonville, Oregon 97417 — **Map Location #1**
541-839-1111 • 800-548-8461
www.sevenfeathers.com

Description: The resort has a 145-room hotel and 31 full-hookup RV spaces. RV registration is at the Security desk in the casino. The heated pool, spa and fitness center at the resort are available to RV guests. Last year's RV rates were $16 for pull-thrus and $14 for back-ins. The casino is open 24 hours daily and has 1,013 slots, 19 pit/table games, live keno, poker room, non-smoking gaming area and bingo six days a week. Food venues include: a 24-hour restaurant with buffet and menu service, a fine dining restaurant, ice cream parlor and a sports bar. Headline entertainment is featured at the convention center. There is an 18-hole golf course at the resort.

Directions & Parking: From Jct. I-5 and Canyonville/Crater Lake (exit 99), the resort is visible from the northbound lanes of the interstate. Seven Feathers is 80 miles south of Eugene, OR. There are 51 designated RV spaces in the dry camping area where overnight parking is permitted. 24-hour shuttle service is provided.

The Mill Resort and Casino
3201 Tremont Avenue (Highway 101)
North Bend, Oregon 97459 — **Map Location #2**
541-756-8800 • 800-953-4800
www.themillcasino.com

Description: On the Oregon coast, the resort has a 115-room/suite hotel. The casino has 550 slots, eight blackjack tables, a smoke-free area and bingo four days a week. Food venues include the waterfront Plank House Restaurant, Timbers Café and Blade Buffet. There is an espresso bar, lounge, gift shop and live music nightly.

Discounts: A buffet discount is extended to Players Club members. Seniors, 55 and older, get 10% off food.

Directions & Parking: The Mill is on US-101 in North Bend, approximately eight miles north of Jct. 42/101. Ample parking is available in the casino lot; overnight is OK. A pet area is provided.

Chinook Winds Gaming Center
1777 NW 44th Street
Lincoln City, Oregon 97367 — **Map Location #3**
541-996-5700 • 888-CHINOOK
www.chinookwindscasino.com

Description: This casino on the beach has 1,200 slots, 12 pit/gaming tables, a poker room and live keno. It has a smoke-free area.

Discounts: Seniors, 55 and older, receive a buffet discount. A Fun Book is given to new Players Club members.

Directions & Parking: From Hwy-101 to Lincoln City, east on Logan St to 44th St, left to the casino. The 30 spaces designated for RVs are on a first-come, first-serve basis. Overnight parking is allowed, but generators may not be used.

Spirit Mountain Casino
27100 SW Salmon River Highway
Grand Ronde, Oregon 97396 — **Map Location #4**
503-879-2350 • 800-760-7977
www.spiritmountain.com

Description: The 24/7 casino has over 1,200 slots, 50 gaming tables, poker room, non-smoking gaming area, bingo and three restaurants. There is a 94-room hotel and video arcade on site.

Discounts: Ask about Fun Books at the Players Services desk.

Directions & Parking: The resort is 60 miles southwest of Portland on Hwy-18. From Portland: Take Hwy-99 west to Hwy-18 west to Grand Ronde. From Salem: Take Hwy-22 west to Hwy-18 to Grand Ronde. There is a designated lot for RV parking and overnight is OK.

Kla-Mo-Ya Casino
3433 Highway 97 North
Cheloquin, Oregon 97624 — **Map Location #6**
541-783-7529 • 888-552-6692
www.klamoya.com

Description: The 24/7 casino has 300 slots from pennies to $5, video poker and keno and live action poker. Dining options include the Still Waters Buffet and Rapids Deli.

Discounts: Senior citizen discount is given at the buffet and there are promotions on Senior Day, every Monday.

Directions: Located on Hwy-97 20 miles north of Klamath Falls. Parking is available for RVs; please check in with Security if you plan to stay overnight.

Eastern Oregon (off I-84)

Wildhorse Resort & Casino & RV Park
72777 Highway 331
Pendleton, Oregon 97801 — **Map Location #5**
541-278-2274 • 800-654-9453
www.wildhorseresort.com

Description: The resort has a 100-room hotel and an RV park. The 100 full-hookup RV sites are walking distance to the casino. There is a heated pool, spa and laundry. Free continental breakfast is served to RV guests. Last year's RV rates were $18–$21. The casino has 650 slots, 16 pit/gaming tables, a poker room, off track betting and live keno. The resort includes four restaurants (one is open 24 hours), an 18-hole championship golf course with clubhouse grill café, cultural museum, teepee village plus indoor and outdoor pools.

Directions: From I-84 exit 216, the resort entrance is .8 mile north of the interstate. The resort is four miles east of Pendleton, Oregon in the northeastern part of the state.

South Dakota

South Dakota's casinos can be found at Indian operated facilities mostly along I-90 and I-29 and in historic Deadwood where there are over 30 small gaming halls.

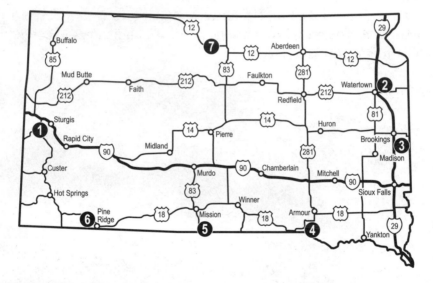

Also, as you travel this state you'll notice "casino" signs at bars, taverns, gas stations, even laundromats. Up to ten video lottery terminals (VLT's) are permitted at some locations. The machines, regulated by the state, are poker, keno, blackjack or bingo.

South Dakota originally limited table game bets to $5 maximum. However, in 2000 the law was changed to raise maximum bets to $100.

Historic Deadwood, page 229

Map	Casino
1	Historic Deadwood, over 30 casinos

Casinos Along I-29, page 232

Central South Dakota, page 234

Northern South Dakota, page 235

Historic Deadwood

The historic mining town of Deadwood, SD is an interesting and unique gaming destination. Deadwood's long history of gambling began when the gold rush of 1876 ushered in the now legendary saloons, dance hall girls and notorious gamblers such as Poker Alice and Wild Bill Hickok. Gambling was officially banned in 1905 but kept going strong until 1947 when it was finally eliminated. In 1989 voters of South Dakota approved legislation to once again open the gaming halls in Deadwood. Limited stakes gambling was authorized with $5 maximum bets. In 2000 the bet limit was raised to $100. Proceeds from gaming go toward historic preservation.

Deadwood is a designated historic landmark and all buildings in the downtown area conform to authentic 1800's architecture. Free walking tours are conducted every day. Deadwood is famous as the place where Wild Bill Hickok was shot to death while playing cards in a saloon. It is said the hand Wild Bill held when he was shot contained two pair, aces and eights, known thereafter as "the dead man's hand." Visitors can actually go to the Old Style Saloon #10 and see the place where Wild Bill met his fate. Wild Bill's chair and other Old West artifacts are on display. During the summer, reenactments are held at 1, 3, 5 and 7pm.

The Sherman Street Parking Lot has free overnight parking for RVs. Trolley service is available to the casinos daily between Memorial Day and mid-September; the fare is 50¢.

Directions to Deadwood: — **Map Location #1** — From I-90 Exit 30, follow Highway 14A into Deadwood, to the third stop light, then left on US-85 and left on to Sherman St for the Sherman Street Parking area. The trolley stop is next to the parking lot.

The 1800's style Deadwood Restoration includes:

B.B. Cody's, 681 Main Street: Family fun stop. 57 slots plus three blackjack tables. Ranch Restaurant, 8am to midnight and kid's arcade.

Best Western Hickok House, 137 Charles Street: Nickel to $5 slots and cozy lounge with beer and wine.

Bodega Bar, 662 Main St, built in 1879, one of Deadwood's landmarks, oldest bar, open 24 hours.

Buffalo Saloon, 658 Main St, where Buffalo Bill Cody ate and drank; 6,900 buffalo nickels on display. 40 slots.

Bullock Express, 633 Main St, hotel and casino. 25 slots. Bullock Express Diner, 6:30am to 9pm.

Bullock Hotel & Casino, 633 Main St, 24 hour gaming, 60 slots. Bully's Restaurant features steak and seafood.

Cadillac Jack's Gaming Resort, 360 Main St, Newest slots and friendly dealers. Hotel with indoor pool, free breakfast.

Celebrity Hotel & Casino, 629 Main St, Open 24/7 with 74 slots. Hotel guests get continental breakfast.

Dakota Frontier, 670 Main St, in historic downtown Deadwood, 60 slots and one table, open 8am–2am.

Deadwood Dick's Saloon & Gaming Hall, 51 Sherman St, Historic building, ten slots, blackjack tables, outdoor patio and antique mall.

Deadwood Gulch Resort, Hwy 85 South, 24 hour gaming. 100 slots, blackjack, video poker. Complimentary drinks to players. Hotel, pool, restaurant 7am-9pm.

Main Street Deadwood Gulch, 560 Main St, Saloon open 9am-2am, 80 slots and lottery tickets.

Fairmont Hotel & Oyster Bar Restaurant, 628 Main St, World-Famous Oyster Bar and Italian restaurant. Gaming 10am-2am. Historic Site over 100 years old.

First Gold Hotel & Gaming, 270 Main St, Blackjack, three-card-poker, 24 hour slots. Complimentary beer and wine to players. Horseshoe Restaurant & Bar, 6am-10pm.

Four Aces, 531 Main St, Free beer and wine for active gamblers. Home of the famous Wild Bill statue. Open 24 hours. Casino in Hampton Inn.

Gold Country Inn Casino, 801 Main St, Casino open 6:30am-midnight. Free drinks to all players. Friendly service.

Gold Dust Gaming, 688 Main St, Open 24/7. Poker, blackjack, slots. Complimentary drinks to players. Casino adjacent to Holiday Inn Express.

Gulches of Fun Casino, Hwy 85 South, 24 hour gaming in a three-casino complex. Blackjack tables.

Hickok's Saloon, 685 Main St, 89 slots, blackjack, three-card poker, nickel parlor. Large kids arcade downstairs.

Lady Luck, 660 Main St, Loose slots, complimentary drinks to players. Located in the same building as Buffalo Saloon.

Lucky 8 Gaming, 196 Cliff St, Open 24 hours, high percentage payback slots. Super 8 motel has indoor pool.

Midnight Star, 677 Main St, 52 slots, six tables, Lil's Sportsbar and Jake's Fine Dining.

Mineral Palace, 605 Main St, Blackjack, poker and 100 slots. Open 24 hours.

Miss Kitty's, 647 Main St, In the heart of Deadwood's Main St, live action games and 100 slots. Two restaurants – Mexican & Chinese.

Mustang Sally's, 634 Main St, Antique slot display. Nickel, quarter, dollar & five-dollar slots.

Old Style Saloon #10, 657 Main St, Where Wild Bill was shot; reenactments four times daily. Single deck blackjack & poker, slots. Live music daily.

Silverado Gaming, 709 Main St, open 24 hours. 225 slots, 16 tables. Grand Buffet at Silverado Restaurant.

Star of the West Casino, 700 Main St, Historic Franklin Hotel, open 24 hours, one of the oldest gaming halls in Deadwood, 80 slots, tables.

Stockade, 654 Main St, Deadwood's largest, oldest original building. Live music, full bar and food service.

Tin Lizzie Gaming, 555 Main St, Gaming in the heart of Deadwood, open 24/7. Lizzies Restaurant 7am-11pm.

Big Dipper Ice Cream, 652 Main St, Old West flavor. Fine coffees, lattes and ice cream.

VFW, 10 Pine St, 9:30am to midnight. Slots, bingo every Monday 6:45pm

Wild West Casino, 622 Main St, Slots and specialty shops. Wild Bill Interpretive Site and home of the Nugget Bar.

Wooden Nickel, 9 Lee St, Open 9am–11pm with 30 slots.

Casinos Along I-29

Dakota Sioux Casino & RV Spaces
16415 Sioux Conifer Road
Watertown, South Dakota 57201 — **Map Location #2**

605-882-2051 • 800-658-4717
www.dakotasioux.com

Description: The casino features over 200 slots, eight blackjack tables ($2 tables on Tuesdays), a five-table poker room and a restaurant, lounge and snack bar. It is open 24/7. There are seven RV spaces in the paved parking lot with electric hookups plus a central dump and fresh water supply. These spaces are free on a first-come, first-serve basis. RVs should register at the guest services desk. There is a hotel on site.

Discounts: Monday is Senior Day with match play and other incentives offered. Daily promotions and drawings are featured for Players Club members.

Directions & Parking: From I-29 exit 185 (Waverly), the casino is four miles west of the interstate.

Royal River Casino & RV Spaces

607 South Veterans Street
Flandreau, South Dakota 57028 — **Map Location #3**
605-997-3746 • 800-833-8666
www.royalrivercasino.com

Description: The casino complex includes a motel and RV park. The 120-room/suite motel has an indoor pool and hot tub. The RV area is located on the south side of the motel and has 20 sites with electric and cable TV plus a central dump and fresh water supply. RV guests are invited to use the motel pool and showers. Last year's RV rate was $10. Check in at the motel. The casino has over 250 slots and eight blackjack/poker tables. The River Bend Restaurant has buffet and menu service morning to night. There is a snack bar in the casino. The entertainment center features live concerts on weekends. There are also free shows in the Royal Room.

Discounts: A Fun Book for seniors 55+ is available on Tuesdays.

Directions & Parking: From I-29 exit 114 go east into Flandreau for 7.6 miles, then right on Veterans St for .4 mile. Free overnight RV parking is also permitted in the casino lot.

Central South Dakota

Fort Randall Casino Hotel & RV Spaces
East Highway 46
Pickstown, South Dakota 57380 — **Map Location #4**
605-487-7871 • 800-362-6333
www.fortrandall.com

Description: Owned and operated by the Yankton Sioux Tribe, there are ten back-in RV spaces with free electric hookups on the west side of the hotel. The hotel has 57 rooms. The casino has 250 slots in all denominations, video poker, eight gaming tables and a separate poker room. There is a $2 minimum at most tables. The casino is open 24/7; tables open at 10am. The casual Directions Restaurant has menu service and a buffet.

Directions & Parking: From I-29 exit 26, take Hwy-50 west for 90 miles into Wagner, then west on Hwy-46 for nine miles to the casino on the right. — or — From I-90 exit 310, south on Hwy-281 for 46 miles, then southeast on US-50 for six miles, then west on Hwy-46 for ten miles.

Rosebud Casino
Highway 83 (SD/NE state line)
Mission, South Dakota 57555 — **Map Location #5**
605-378-3800 • 800-786-7673
www.rosebudcasino.com

Description: Located at the state line, the casino is open 24 hours daily and has over 300 slots, from pennies to $5, plus five blackjack tables and a poker room. Bingo is held every day. The Rosebud Room Restaurant features prime rib buffet every night. There is a deli and gift shop. The modern Quality Inn hotel has 60 rooms.

Directions & Parking: From I-90 exit 192, south on Hwy-83 for 67 miles to the Nebraska state line. (Note there are some steep grades on Hwy-83). The parking area for large vehicles in on the east side of the lot; overnight RV parking is OK.

Prairie Wind Casino
Highway 18
Pine Ridge, South Dakota 57770 — **Map Location #6**
605-867-6300 • 800-705-9463
www.prairiewindcasino.com

Description: The 24-hour casino has 250 slots, live blackjack and three-card poker. Blackjack tournaments are held monthly, slot tournaments weekly. The restaurant is open 7am–10pm with daily buffet specials as well as menu service. The facility is owned and operated by the Oglala Sioux Tribe on the Pine Ridge Indian Reservation just north of the Nebraska state line.

Directions & Parking: The casino is 12 miles east of Oelrichs on Hwy-18, 12 miles west of Oglala. Free overnight parking is permitted for self-contained RVs.

Northern South Dakota

Grand River Casino & RV Park
Highway 12
Mobridge, South Dakota 57601 — **Map Location #7**
605-845-7104 • 800-475-3321
www.grandrivercasino.com

Description: Owned by the Standing Rock Sioux Tribe, the casino facility has a 40-room hotel and an RV park. There are 250 slots, live blackjack and live poker in the casino. Tables open at 3pm daily. Dining options include a buffet and sandwich bar. The RV park has 70 sites and ten cabins all with electric and access to fish cleaning stations. There is fresh water, a central dump and a convenience store where bait, tackle and sundries are available.

Directions: Located on Hwy-12, two miles west of Mobridge.

Washington

The State of Washington is home to the Northwest's largest Indian gaming facility, the beautiful Tulalip Casino, located near I-5 between Seattle and Vancouver.

There are 29 federally recognized Tribes in the State of Washington; 27 of them have gaming compacts with the state. This section includes:

- 12 casinos in Western Washington, all accessible from I-5.
- One casino in South-Central Washington accessible from I-82, and
- Three casinos in Eastern Washington convenient to I-90.

Most casino machines in Washington are cashless; players must buy slot tickets from the cashier or from machines located around the gaming floor.

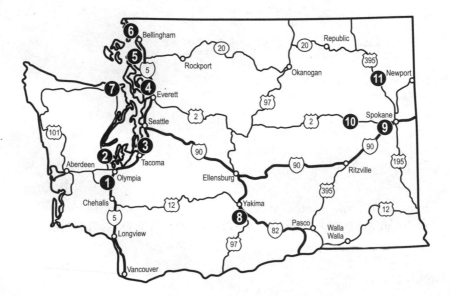

Western Washington (south of Seattle), page 237

Western Washington (north of Seattle), page 240

Central Washington, page 244

Eastern Washington (off I-90), page 245

Western Washington – south of Seattle

Lucky Eagle Casino
12888 188th Avenue SW
Rochester, Washington 98579 — **Map Location #1**

360-273-2000 • 800-720-1788
www.luckyeagle.com

Description: This 75,000 square foot casino has over 500 slots, 26 pit/ table games, a separate keno area, 5X odds on craps every day, non-smoking slots in a separate clean-air room and bingo. Food venues include the Grand Buffet everyday, Golden Eagle Steakhouse open every night from 5pm for dinner, Center Stage Grille, open daily at 11am and the Sidewalk Deli in the bingo hall. Live entertainment is featured in the Cabaret Room on Friday and Saturday nights. Casino hours are 10am–4am/6am (Fri–Sat).

Directions & Parking: The casino is located 26 miles south of Olympia. From I-5 exit 88, go west on Hwy-12 for 7.7 miles, then left on Anderson Rd for .8 mile, then left on 188th Ave for .2 mile. There are 20 RV sites with electric hookups available on a first-come, first-serve basis. Last year's charge was $8 per night for those with a Players Card (free hookups for qualified players).

Little Creek Casino
West 91 Highway 108
Shelton, Washington 98584 — **Map Location #2**
360-427-7711 • 800-667-7711
www.little-creek.com

Description: The casino has 612 cashless slots, 22 gaming tables and three restaurants. Casino hours are 10am–4am/6am (Fri–Sat). There is a 92-room hotel at the casino and a gas station/convenience store is across the street.

Discounts: Ask about senior specials on Tuesdays and Wednesdays.

Directions & Parking: From I-5 in Olympia, exit 104, north on US-101 for five miles (follow signs to Port Angeles/Shelton) and continue north on US-101 for another 7.5 miles. Exit US-101 between mileposts 353 & 354 (at Hwy-108). The casino is next to the southbound lanes of the highway and can be seen from both sides, but there are no casino signs at the exits. The designated parking area for RVs is on the west side of the parking lot. Overnight is OK.

Red Wind Casino
12819 Yelm Highway
Olympia, Washington 98513 — **Map Location #3**
360-412-5000 • 866-946-2444

Description: Located on the Nisqually Reservation, the expanded casino has 600 slots and 25 gaming tables plus a buffet restaurant, a deli and a steakhouse for fine dining. Hours are 9am–5am daily.

Discounts: Fun books are available at the promotions booth. Senior discounts for 55 and older are given Monday through Friday.

Directions & Parking: From I-5 exit 111, go east on Hwy-510 (Marvin Road) for 1.7 mile. At the roundabout, turn left to continue on Hwy-510 east for six miles. RV parking is across from the casino building. Overnight parking is permitted.

Emerald Queen Casino Riverboat
2102 Alexander Avenue
Tacoma, Washington 98421 — **Map Location #3**
206-594-7777 • 888-831-7655
www.emeraldqueen.com

Description: This facility has two casino areas: the riverboat has keno and the shoreside building has 1,000 slots, nine tables and a separate high limits area. The Lafayette Restaurant, open from 11am–midnight, features Asian specialties. Casino hours are 10am–6am daily.

Directions & Parking: From I-5 exit 137, west on 54th Ave E, then left on to Hwy-99 (Pacific Hwy) south for 1.1 mile, then right on Alexander Ave for two miles. RVs should park in the overflow lot at the east end of the casino building. Overnight parking is permitted.

Emerald Queen Casino at I-5
2024 East 29th Street
Tacoma, Washington 98404 — **Map Location #3**
888-831-7655
www.emeraldqueen.com

Description: The casino features over 1,500 slots, 41 pit/gaming tables, a clean-air separate non-smoking area, keno lounge, a deli, bar and International Restaurant & Buffet. Headline entertainment is featured at the EQC I-5 Showroom.

Directions & Parking: The casino can be seen from the northbound lanes of I-5 at exit 135. From southbound: exit at #135, turn left at the first light, drive under the interstate and make an immediate left. Stay in the right lane for about a mile and watch for the casino entrance on your right. From northbound: exit at #135 and go straight through the traffic light. Bear right at the Puyallup sign, go about one mile and look for the casino entrance on the right. RVs should park in the overflow area or on the perimeter of the main lot. Overnight parking is permitted.

Muckleshoot Casino
2402 Auburn Way South
Auburn, Washington 98002 — **Map Location #3**
253-804-4444 • 800-804-4944
www.muckleshootcasino.com

Description: Owned and operated by the Muckleshoot Indian Tribe, the casino has 2,000 slots, 70 pit/gaming tables, a poker room and a non-smoking section with slots and tables. Food venues include The Picese Seafood Buffet, The Island Deli, Kookaburra's, The Muckleshoot Restaurant with a Noodle Bar, The Sweet Shoppe and Banquet Rooms for groups from 25–300. Live entertainment is featured nightly in Club Galaxy.

Discounts: Senior Brunch every Saturday for $5.95.

Directions & Parking: From I-5 exit 142 (Auburn), Hwy-18 east for 4.2 miles to Auburn Way exit. Then Hwy-164 east for 1.8 mile to the casino on the left. RV parking is in the west lot. Please obtain a Players Club card and register with Security if you plan to stay overnight.

Western Washington – north of Seattle

Tulalip Casino
10200 Quil Ceda Boulevard

Tulalip, Washington 98271 — **Map Location #4**
360-651-1111 • 888-272-1111
www.tulalipcasino.com

Description: The 227,000 square-foot gaming facility – the largest in the state – has 2,000 video slots, 49 tables, four restaurants and a High Roller Room with ten gaming tables. There is a separate non-smoking area. The lovely casino has a vaulted ceiling over the 100-foot entryway with a hand painted mural depicting the life of the salmon. The main casino floor has a spectacular center dome. Casino hours are: 10am–6am/ 24hours (Fri–Sun). The casino attracts three million visitors annually.

Directions & Parking: From I-5 exit 200, follow casino signs. The casino complex is visible from the southbound lanes of the interstate. RV parking is on the west side of the casino and overnight parking is permitted.

Swinomish Northern Lights Casino & RV Park
837 Casino Drive
Anacortes, Washington 98221 — **Map Location #5**
360-293-2691
www.swinomishcasino.com

Description: The RV park behind the casino has 35 full hookup sites with cable TV and Internet connection. Last year's rates were from $17. RV guests should register in the casino gift shop. The friendly casino has 340 slots, 15 gaming tables, an 11-table poker room, separate keno area, OTB in the summer and bingo every day. Food venues include the pretty Salmon Café, open morning to night with both buffet and menu service and a deli in the bingo hall. The Starlight Lounge has entertainment (including standup comics) on Fridays and live music on Saturdays. Casino hours are: 11am–4am/6am (Fri–Sat).

Discounts: New Players Club members get a Fun Book. Senior Appreciation $2.99 Buffet is offered on Tuesdays.

Directions & Parking: From I-5 exit 230, take Hwy-20 west for 8.5

miles. The casino can be seen on the north side of the highway as you cross the bridge from the mainland to Fidalgo Island at the Swinomish Channel.

Skagit Valley Casino Resort
5984 North Darrk Lane
Bow, Washington 98232 — **Map Location #5**
360-724-7777 • 877-2 SKAGIT
www.theskagit.com

Description: The casino features over 650 cashless slots, 30 gaming tables and a keno lounge. The Market Buffet Grille features international themed buffets, Saturday breakfast buffet and Sunday brunch. The Moon Beach fine dining restaurant is open every night for dinner. There is a deli in the casino. Hours are: 9am–3am/5am (Fri–Sat). A 103-room hotel (with conference rooms) is connected to the casino. An outdoor concert series every summer features headline entertainment.

Discounts: Senior discounts are given on Mondays.

Directions & Parking: From I-5 exit 236, take Bow Hill Rd to Darrk Lane. The casino can be seen from the interstate. RVs should park in the lot designated for oversized vehicles if staying for a short time. If you plan to stay overnight, park in the adjacent Thousand Trails campground (shuttle service available). Last year's fee of $24 per night included a two-for-one coupon at the casino buffet and other casino incentives. *Note*: Free overnight parking for RVs is NOT allowed in the casino lot.

Nooksack River Casino
5048 Mt. Baker Highway
Deming, Washington 98244 — **Map Location #6**
360-592-5472 • 877-935-9300
www.nooksackcasino.com

Description: The 22,000 square foot casino has over 400 slots, 12 gaming tables, a poker room and separate keno area. The Everyday

Great Buffet has a champagne brunch on Sundays. A Bar & Grille is located at the Lounge, where live entertainment is featured on Friday and Saturday. Casino hours are: 10am–3am/6am (Fri–Sat). The Nooksack Market Center with a deli, pizza and full service bakery is located next door to the casino.

Directions & Parking: From I-5 exit 255, go east on Hwy-542 (Sunset Drive - turns into Mt. Baker Hwy) for 13 miles to the casino on the right. Nine free RV spaces (no electric) are on the east side of the casino; five RV back-in spaces with electric are on the south side of the parking lot. Last year's charge for electric was $10. Free overnight parking is OK in the lot.

Silver Reef Casino
4876 Haxton Way
Ferndale, Washington 98248 — **Map Location #6**
360-383-0777 • 866-383-0777
www.silverreefcasino.com

Description: Located seven miles north of Bellingham and just below the Canadian border, the 28,000 square foot casino has more than 330 slots and ten pit/gaming tables. Food venues include the Red River Café, Gold Rush Bakery & Deli, Portage Bay Bar & Lounge and the Steakhouse for fine dining. Live entertainment appears in the pavilion. Hours are: 10am–4am/6 am (Fri–Sat).

Directions & Parking: From I-5 exit 260, go west on Slater Rd for 3.7 miles, then turn left on Haxton Way into the casino. RVs should park in the south lot; overnight parking is permitted.

7 Cedars Casino
270756 Highway 101
Sequim, Washington 98382 — **Map Location #7**
360-683-7777 • 800-4-LUCKY-7
www.7cedarscasino.com

Description: The pretty casino, located on the north side of the Olympic

Peninsula directly on US-101 in Sequim, is open daily from 10am–1am/3am (Fri–Sat). It has over 200 slots, ten gaming tables, a separate clean-air non smoking section and Off Track Betting. The Salish Room Restaurant has both buffet and menu service and there is full menu service in the Totem Lounge in the casino. Bingo is held daily and live entertainment is featured in the Cabaret Room.

Discounts: Lunch buffet, noon–3pm, is $2.99 with a $5 slot coupon buy. A daily $5.05 steak special is on the menu all day at the Totem Lounge. Other restaurant specials are offered throughout the week.

Directions & Parking: The casino can be reached by ferry from Seattle, or by driving on US-101 north into Sequim from the Olympia area. Free overnight parking is available for RVs. Please check in at the casino if you plan to stay overnight.

Central Washington

Yakama Nation Legends Casino
580 Fort Road
Toppenish, Washington 98948 — **Map Location #8**
509-865-8800 • 877-7-COME-11
www.yakamalegends.com

Description: Owned and operated by the Yakama Nation, the 45,000 square foot casino in south-central Washington has 800 slots, 26 pit/gaming tables, a poker room, live keno and bingo six days a week. Food venues include Mountain View Buffet and a deli in the casino. Hours are 9am–4am/5am (Fri–Sat). Table games open at 10am. Special outdoor events (concerts, rodeos, pow-wows) are held during the summer. There is no hotel at this location. The Yakama Nation's modern RV park is located a short distance from the casino and is next to the Yakama National Heritage Center.

Discounts: Out of state visitors will receive a Fun Book and souvenirs. Tuesday is Senior Day with free breakfast and coupon books with lots of free stuff for senior citizens.

Directions & Parking: From I-82 exit 50, east on Hwy-22 (through the town of Toppenish) for three miles, turn right on Hwy-97 (second light) for one-half mile, then turn left on to Fort Rd for one-half mile to the casino on the left. Ample free RV parking is available in the casino lot. Please notify Security if you are staying overnight.

Eastern Washington (off I-90)

Northern Quest Casino
100 North Hayford Road
Airway Heights, Washington 99001 — **Map Location #9**
509-242-7000 • 888-603-7051
www.northernquest.net

Description: Located near Spokane, the casino is open daily 9am–5am. It has 1,000 slots from pennies to $5 and 30 pit/table games. There is an eight-table non-smoking poker room and a separate non-smoking gaming area with slots and tables. Food venues include a buffet restaurant, 24-hour coffee shop, a noodle bar and 24-hour deli. There is also a lounge with a large screen TV.

Discounts: Seniors receive buffet discounts if 55 and older.

Directions & Parking: From I-90 exit 277, west on Hwy-2 for four miles, right on Hayford Road for one mile to the casino on the left. RVs should follow signs to the designated area. Overnight parking is permitted for self-contained RVs.

Two Rivers Casino & RV Resort
6828-B Highway 25 South
Davenport, Washington 99122 — **Map Location #10**
509-722-4000 • 800-722-4031
www.tworiverscasinoandresort.com

Description: Owned and operated by the Spokane Tribe, the casino resort has an RV park that offers beautiful views from 100 sites with full hookups. All sites and roads are paved. The park has a swimming beach at Lake Roosevelt, laundry, convenience store and deli. There is also a 260-slip marina. Last year's RV rates were $19–$23 and the park is open all year. Early reservations are strongly suggested during warm weather months. The casino is walking distance and has 300 slots, video poker, six tables and a snack bar. Casino hours are 8am–12:30am/24 hours (Fri–Sat). There is no hotel at this location.

Discounts: The RV park gives $5 in casino match play per person per day. Special rates are in effect in December and January.

Directions: From I-90 exit 277, west on US-2 for 30 miles, then north on SR-25 for 23.5 miles (some steep grades and a narrow bridge). RVs who want to boondock in the casino lot must check with Security. There is a $5 fee for use of the dump station by those not staying in the RV park.

Chewelah Casino
2555 Smith Road
Chewelah, Washington 99109 – **Map Location #11**
509-935-6167 • 800-322-2788

Description: The casino has 400 slots and seven pit/table games on a 22,000 square foot gaming floor. The restaurant has buffet and menu service. Casino hours are 7am–2am/24 hrs weekends. There are 20 RV sites with electric and water (no dump station) available for $10 per night. There is no hotel at this location.

Discounts: Senior discounts are offered on Wednesdays. A Fun Book is distributed on Fridays.

Directions & Parking: From I-90 exit 281, go north on US-395 for approximately 40 miles. The casino can be seen on the east side of the highway. Free overnight parking is also permitted for RVs.

Note: The smaller Double Eagle Casino is next to the main casino; it has additional slots and a deli.

West Virginia

There are four pari-mutuel facilities with slots – known as "racinos" – in West Virginia. Two are at dog tracks and two are at horse tracks. The machines at the racinos are referred to as VLTs (video lottery terminals) because they are regulated by the state's lottery commission. They include traditional slots as well as video poker, video blackjack and video keno. Maximum allowable bet on any machine is $2.

Three of the four facilities in West Virginia are RV-friendly. They are listed below. (Note that Wheeling Island does not allow overnight parking for RVs).

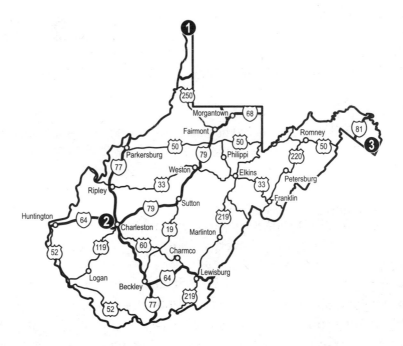

Racinos, page 248

Map   *Casino*
1   Mountaineer Race Track & Gaming Resort
2   Tri-State Racetrack & Gaming Center
3   Charles Town Races & Slots

Racinos

Mountaineer Race Track & Gaming Resort
State Route 2
Chester, West Virginia 26034 — **Map Location #1**
304-387-2400 • 800-489-8192
www.mtrgaming.com

Description: The resort includes an 80,000 square foot casino with 3,200 slots, a 359-room hotel, spa and fitness center and an 18-hole golf course. Food venues include 12 restaurants. Live thoroughbred racing is held year-round. Casino hours are: 7:30am–3:30am & 10am–3:30am (Sun).

Directions & Parking: From Weirton, West Virginia, follow US-2 north for 15 miles to Mountaineer. The south lot (trackside) is designated for large vehicles. Overnight parking is OK for RVs.

Tri-State Racetrack & Gaming Center
1 Greyhound Lane
Cross Lanes, West Virginia 25356 — **Map Location #2**
304-776-1000 • 800-224-9683

Description: The 30,000 square foot casino has 1,600 VLTs and daily racing simulcasting. Food venues include a deli/grill and full service American restaurant. Live greyhound racing takes place daily, year-round except Tues and Sun. Casino hours are 11am–3am & 1pm–3am (Sun).

Directions & Parking: From I-64 use exit 47 or 47A. Tri-State can be seen from the interstate. RVs should park in back of the casino building. Check in with Security if you plan to stay overnight.

Charles Town Races & Slots
US-340, Flowing Springs Road
Charles Town, West Virginia 25414 — **Map Location #3**
304-725-7001 • 800-795-7001
www.pngaming.com

Description: The casino has 3,500 slots and daily simulcasting of horse and dog racing. The six-furlongs horse track features live thoroughbred racing. Food venues include Silverado Buffet, Longhorn Deli/grill, a food court, the elegant Skyline Terrace and a lounge. Casino hours are 7am–3:30am/10am–3:30am (Sun).

Directions & Parking: From I-81 exit 5, follow Rt-51 east for 12 miles. RVs should park on the back end of F Lot (near the railroad tracks). Overnight parking is permitted for self-contained RVs.

Wisconsin

In 1987, when Wisconsin voters approved the creation of a state lottery, they also gave Wisconsin's Indian Tribes the right to establish casino-type gambling (permissible only in states already allowing Class III gaming). Since then, a number of tribes, including the Ho-Chunk, Ojibwa, Mohican and Potawatomi, opened casinos that provide substantial economic benefits to reservation communities.

Wisconsin's Indian tribes offer casino gaming in locations throughout the state. Included in this section are casinos

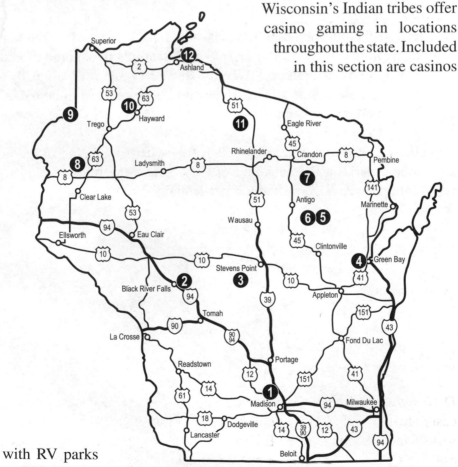

with RV parks or RV spaces and 24-hour casinos that offer free overnight parking. Excluded from these listings are facilities that are not practical for RVs because they are too small or too remote or difficult for a large vehicle to access.

Southern Wisconsin, page 251

Northern Wisconsin, page 253

Southern Wisconsin

Ho-Chunk Casino Hotel
S3214 Highway 12
Baraboo, Wisconsin 53913 — **Map Location #1**
608-356-6210 • 800-746-2486
www.ho-chunk.com

Description: Located in The Dells, a popular vacation area, the 24-hour casino features 2,500 slot machines, 47 blackjack tables and bingo. Food venues include: Stand Rock Buffet restaurant, Copper Oak Steakhouse, Sunrise Cliffs Café, concessions and snack bar. There is a 315-room/ suite hotel and a convention center on site. Live entertainment is featured on weekends in the Upper Dells Ballroom.

Discounts: Discount smoke shop at the resort.

Directions & Parking: From I-90/94 exit 92, take Hwy-12 south for four miles to the casino. RVs should park in the back parking lot. Free overnight parking is available; check in with Security.

Majestic Pines Hotel & Casino & RV Spaces
W9010 State Road 54 East
Black River Falls, Wisconsin 54615 — **Map Location #2**
715-284-9098 • 800-657-4621
www.mpcwin.com

Description: The casino has 600 slots and eight blackjack tables (both standard shoe and double deck) with $3 minimums on weekdays. Restaurants include the Mystic Pines Buffet and a snack bar. The casino is open 24 hours every day from Memorial Day to Labor Day. From Labor Day to Memorial Day it is open weekdays 8am–2am/24hrs (Fri–Sat). There is a 60-room hotel with an indoor pool on site.

Discounts: Players Club card holders get 10% off buffets.

Directions & Parking: From I-94 exit 116, go east for four miles on Hwy-54. RV parking is in the east parking lot. There are a few spaces with free electric hookups at the northeast end of the lot. Overnight RV parking is OK.

Rainbow Casino & RV Spaces
949 County Road G
Nekoosa, Wisconsin 54457 — **Map Location #3**
715-886-4560 • 800-782-4560
www.rbcwin.com

Description: The casino has 650 slots in denominations from pennies to $5, blackjack and poker tables and bingo Wed-Sun. Food venues include The Grille, a full service restaurant in a rustic atmosphere, and a snack bar. There is a smoke and gift shop featuring Native American gifts. Casino hours are 8am–2am/24hrs (Fri–Sat).

Discounts: Senior citizen specials on Thursdays if 55+

Directions & Parking: From I-39 exit 136, take Hwy-73 west into Nekoosa, then turn left on County Road G. The casino is about four miles south of Nekoosa on County Road G. There are eight RV spaces in the parking lot with free electric hookups.

Oneida Bingo & Casino & RV Spaces
2020/2100 Airport Drive
Green Bay, Wisconsin 54313 — **Map Location #4**
920-494-4500 • 800-238-4263
www.oneidabingoandcasino.net

Description: Two casinos and a 414-room/suite hotel are located on the property. The casinos have 2,800 reel slot and video machines and 60 blackjack tables with limits from $3 to $200. A high stakes area is located in the main casino. Five restaurants include the buffet and fine dining. There is bingo hall that seats over 800. The casinos are open 24 hours.

Directions & Parking: From I-43 north exit 180, or from US-41 north, take Rt-172 west to Airport Rd. Several RV parking spaces with free electric hookups can be found along the road near the smaller casino at the back of the property.

Northern Wisconsin

Menominee Casino, Hotel & RV Park
Highway 47/55 – Box 760
Keshena, Wisconsin 54135 — **Map Location #5**
715-799-3600 • 800-343-7778
www.menomineecasinoresort.com

Description: Located on the Menominee Indian Reservation, the RV parking area has 60 spaces. RV guests should register at the hotel front desk. Last year's rates were $15 for sites with water and electric and $10 for sites without electric. RV guests may use the hotel pool, spa and sauna. The spacious casino has 850 slots, 12 blackjack tables (double deck pitch games and five-deck shoes), a poker room and live entertainment in the lounge. The Forest Island Buffet is open morning to night and the casino is open 24/7.

Discounts: Registered RV guests (two per vehicle) receive $5 match play per day. Seniors, 55 and older, are given $5 match play on Tuesdays.

Directions: Located 40 miles northwest of Green Bay. From US-41 go west on Hwy-29 to junction with Hwy-47 at Shawano, then five miles north on Hwy-47.

Mohican North Star Casino & RV Park
W12180 County Road A
Bowler, Wisconsin 54416 — **Map Location #6**
715-793-4090 • 800-952-0195
715-787-2751 (RV park)
www.mohicannorthstar.com

Description: Owned and operated by the Mohican Nation, the facility has a campground and casino – no hotel. The campground features 57 wooded sites with full hookups, telephone access, picnic tables and 24-hour security. It is walking distance to the casino. Camping fees in 2005 were from $15 per night with higher rates on weekends and holidays. There are over 1,000 slots and 18 pit/gaming tables in the somewhat crowded casino. Hours are 8am–2am/24hrs (Fri–Sat). The RV park and casino are open all year. There is a convenience store on site.

Directions: Located 50 miles northwest of Green Bay. From US-41 in Green Bay go west on Hwy-29 (MP 217) to CR-U north for two miles, then take CR-A for seven miles to the casino. —or— From I-39 exit 187, east on Hwy-29 for 23.6 miles to CR-Q north for 8.8 miles (narrow two-lane road over hills through scenic farmland). Note the road name changes to CR-D. At CR-A turn left for six miles to the casino.

Mole Lake Regency Casino
Highway 55
Mole Lake, Wisconsin 54520 — **Map Location #7**

715-478-5290 • 800-236-9466
www.molelake.com

Description: The casino has 500 slots from pennies up, progressives and video keno. Blackjack tables open daily at 3pm and bingo is held Fri–Tue. There is a café open daily for three meals, Windtalkers Lounge and the Bistro for fine dining evenings (closed Wed–Thu). Casino hours are 10am–2am/3am (Fri–Sat).

Discounts: Senior Day on Wednesdays features match play for those 50 and older.

Directions: The casino is located seven miles southwest of Crandon on Hwy-55. Free overnight parking is permitted for self-contained RVs.

Potawatomi Bingo / Northern Lights Casino
Highway 32
Wabeno, Wisconsin 54566 — **Map Location #7**
715-473-2021 • 800-487-9522
www.cartercasino.com

Description: The 12,000 square-foot casino is open 9am–1am/24hrs (Fri–Sat) and has slots, progressives, video poker, live blackjack and three-card poker, roulette and bingo (Wed–Sun). The Fire Keeper Café features daily specials. There is a 99-room/suite lodge, 24-hour gas station and convenience store.

Discounts: Weekly specials on Senior Day every Thursday.

Directions: Located 85 miles north of Green Bay on Hwy-32. There is ample parking space for RVs. Please check in with Security if you plan to stay overnight.

St. Croix Casino & RV Park
777 U.S. Highway 8 West
Turtle Lake, Wisconsin 54889 — **Map Location #8**

715-986-4777 • 800-846-8946
www.stcroixcasino.com

Description: Located in northwestern Wisconsin, the resort includes a 95,000 square-foot casino, a 160-room/suite hotel and an RV park that is open May to October. The RV park has 18 campsites with water and electric, picnic tables and barbeque grills. Laundry and shower facilities are in the RV office. Last year's RV rates were $20 per night; $125 per week. The Vegas-style casino has 1,100 slots from pennies to dollars, 23 blackjack tables plus craps and roulette on a spacious gaming floor. There is a separate non-smoking slots area, 12-table poker room open 24/7 and a high stakes area. The Me-Ki-Noc Restaurant and the Buffet are open morning to night.

Directions & Parking: The resort is on US-8 (a major east/west route in Wisconsin), one mile west of Hwy-63 —or— From I-35 in Minnesota take exit 132 and go east on US 8; cross the Mississippi River into Wisconsin and continue 20 miles on US-8 to the casino. Free RV parking is available across from the casino on Hwy-8 in the Barn Lot, where there is a heated bus waiting area. Shuttle service is provided.

Hole In The Wall Casino & RV Park
30223 State Road 35
Danbury, Wisconsin 54830 — **Map Location #9**
715-656-3444 • 800-238-8946
www.stcroixcasino.com/HoleInTheWall

Description: The Western-themed complex includes a 46-room hotel, RV park and casino. The 35-site RV park is nestled in the pines behind the casino and each site has electric, picnic table and fire ring. RV guests may also use the swimming pool, sauna and jacuzzi in the hotel. The Loose Change Café is open for three meals daily. There is a smoke and gift shop on site. The friendly casino has ten blackjack tables, roulette, craps and 315 slot machines. Hours are 8am–2am/4am (Fri–Sat).

Directions: From I-35 exit 183 in MN, east on SR-48 and cross the river

into Wisconsin. Follow Hwy-35 north to junction of Hwy-77, then north
.1 mile on Hwy-35.

LCO Casino, Lodge & Convention Center

13767 West County Road B
Hayward, Wisconsin 54843 — **Map Location #10**
715-634-5643 • 800-526-2274
www.lcocasino.com

Description: Located in northwestern Wisconsin, an area renowned for
its forested scenic beauty and trophy fishing waters, the resort features a
61-room/suite lodge and a 35,000 square-foot casino with 600 slots,
eight blackjack tables and bingo six days a week. Food venues include
the LCO Buffet and Restaurant open daily 11am–3am, Wigwam Café
and a sports bar. Casino hours are 9am–4am daily.

Directions & Parking: From US-63 in Hayward, take Hwy-27 south for
.5 mile to CR-B, then east for four miles to the casino. Free overnight
parking is available for RVs in the area east of the casino building.

Lake of the Torches Resort Casino & RV Park

510 Old Abe Road
Lac du Flambeau, Wisconsin 54538 — **Map Location #11**
715-588-7070 • 800-25-TORCH
www.lakeofthetorches.com

Description: The RV park, open May 1 to Oct 1, is located one mile
north of the casino on Hwy-47. It has 72 blacktop sites (17 with full
hookups), central dump station, showers and laundry. All sites are
lakefront. On-call shuttle service is available to the casino. 2005 daily
rate was from $24; weekly rate is $138. The 101-room/suite hotel and
conference center are rustic Northwoods style. The resort is situated
near a ten-lake chain in northern Wisconsin with boating and fishing at
lakes that have trophy size muskies, walleyes and bass. Canoe rental
with guide service is available. The unique casino-in-the-round features

Native American-themed murals on the rounded walls. It has 900 slots at various levels of play and 12 blackjack tables. Food venues include a buffet restaurant, fish fries every day and a food court just off the gaming floor. The casino is open 24/7.

Directions: From I-39 in Wausau, continue north on US-51 to the town of Woodruff (Jct. Hwy-47). Turn left on Hwy-47 and continue west for 12 miles to the casino. Free overnight parking for RVs is available on the level gravel lot across the street from the casino next to the gas station.

Bad River Lodge & Casino & RV Spaces
123 Maple Street, State Highway 2
Odanah, Wisconsin 54861 — **Map Location #12**
715-682-7121 • 800-777-7449
www.badriver.com

Description: Owned and operated by the Bad River Band of the Lake Superior Tribe of Chippewa Indians, the resort offers 20 free RV spaces with electric and water and a dump station. There is a gas station, IGA market, post office and mini casino at the convenience store. The hotel has 50 rooms. The main casino has over 400 slots, eight pit/gaming tables, $2 shoe games, $3 pitch games and $5 blackjack free play. The Manomin Restaurant is open from 7am–9pm. There is live music and comedy night on weekends. RV spaces are walking distance to the casino and the store. Casino hours are 8am–2am/4am (Fri–Sat).

Discounts: First time visitors get $5 in casino cash tokens. A 99-cent breakfast is offered daily at the restaurant. Buy ten gallons of gas and get $5 in casino cash.

Directions: Located near Lake Superior ten miles east of Ashland on US-2. The RV spaces are first-come, first-serve.

Appendix A

Casinos With Full Service RV Parks, Campgrounds or Electric Hookups

The state-by-state list below includes casinos that have RV parks or campgrounds as a part of their facility. Casinos that offer parking spaces with electric hookups are also listed here and identified with an asterisk (*). Some have a nominal charge for the electric hookup. Listings are arranged alphabetically by city.

Arizona

City	Casino Name	Nearest Highway	Page
Fountain Hills	Fort McDowell	SR-87 (Beeline)	28
Mohave Valley	Spirit Mountain	I-40 exit 1	32
Pinetop	Hon-Dah	Hwy 260 & 73	27
San Carlos	Apache Gold	Jct US-70/US-60	26

California

City	Casino Name	Nearest Highway	Page
Havasu Landing	Havasu Landing	I-40 exit 144	44
Lakeport	Konocti Vista	US-101 exit 555B	49
Oroville	Feather Falls	CA-65	51
Temecula	Pechanga	I-15 Indio exit	35

Colorado

City	Casino Name	Nearest Highway	Page
Towaoc	Ute Mountain	US-160/US-666	61

Idaho

City	Casino Name	Nearest Highway	Page
Lewiston	Clearwater	I-90 exit 12	72
Worley	Coeur D'Alene *	I-90 exit 12	71

Illinois

City	Casino Name	Nearest Highway	Page
East St. Louis	Casino Queen	I-70/I-55 exit 2A	76
Joliet	Empress	I-80, exit 130	75

Iowa

City	Casino Name	Nearest Highway	Page
Dubuque	Diamond Jo *	Route 20	86
Osceola	Lakeside Resort	I-35, exit 34	89
Sloan	Winnevegas *	I-29 exit 127	91
Tama	Meskwaki *	I-80 exit 191	90

Kansas

City	Casino Name	Nearest Highway	Page
Horton	Golden Eagle	US-75/SR-20	95
Mayetta	Harrah's	US-75	95
Powhattan	Sac & Fox *	US-75	96
White Cloud	White Cloud *	SR-7	97

Louisiana

City	Casino Name	Nearest Highway	Page
Bossier City	Isle of Capri	I-20 exit, 20A	108
Charanton	Grand Cypress	I-10 exit 103A	100

Kinder	Grand Coushatta	I-10 exit 44	101
Lake Charles	Isle of Capri *	I-10 exit 27	107
Marksville	Paragon	I-49/Alexandria	102

Michigan

City	Casino Name	Nearest Highway	Page
Baraga	Ojibwa	US-41 in Baraga	113
Brimley	Bay Mills	I-75 exit 386	114
Harris	Island Resort	Hwy-2 & 41	116
Manistee	Little River	US-31	119
Manistique	Kewadin	I-75 exit 344B	117
Marquette	Ojibwa *	MI-28 east of US 41	113
Peshawbestown	Leelanau Sands *	On MI-22	118
Sault St Marie	Kewadin	I-75 exit 348/353	115
Watersmeet	Lac Vieux	US 45 North	112

Minnesota

City	Casino Name	Nearest Highway	Page
Cass Lake	Palace Casino *	I-35 exit 250	128
Hinckley	Grand Casino	I-35 exit 183	126
Mahnomen	Shooting Star	I-94 exit 60	128
Morton	Jackpot Junction	I-90 exit 73	123
Prior Lake	Mystic Lake	I-35W exit 1	124
Red Wing	Treasure Island	US-61/CR-18	125
Tower	Fortune Bay	Hwy-1/169 Minnesota	129
Walker	Northern Lights	Jct. Hwys-371&200	127

Mississippi

City	Casino Name	Nearest Highway	Page
Robinsonville	Grand Casino	I-55 exit 280	134
Robinsonville	Sam's Town	I-55 exit 280	136

| Robinsonville | Hollywood | I-55 exit 280 | 135 |
| Vicksburg | Isle of Capri | I-20 exit 1A | 140 |

Missouri

City	Casino Name	Nearest Highway	Page
Caruthersville	Casino Aztar	I-55 exit 19	146
La Grange	Mark Twain *	US-61	144

Nevada

City	Casino Name	Nearest Highway	Page
Amargosa Valley	Longstreet	US-95	176
Beatty	Burro Casino	On US-95	176
Carson City	Pinon Plaza	US 50	174
Elko	Gold Country	I-80 exit 303	180
Indian Springs	Indian Springs	US-95	178
Jackpot	Cactus Pete's	I-80 exit 352	183
Las Vegas	Arizona Charlie's	I-515 exit 70	160
Las Vegas	California Casino	I-15/93/95	162
Las Vegas	Circus Circus	I-15 Sahara exit	159
Las Vegas	Sam's Town	Jct. 93/95	161
Laughlin	Avi	I-40 River Rd.	165
Laughlin	Don Laughlin's	SR-163	164
Mesquite	CasaBlanca	I-15 exit 120	167
Mesquite	Oasis	I-15 exit 120	167
Minden	Carson Valley	On US-395	174
Pahrump	Saddle West	SR-160	177
Pahrump	Terrible's	SR-160	177
Primm	Primm Resorts	I-15 at CA line	163
Reno	Reno Hilton	I-80/US 395	170
Reno	Bordertown	I-80/US 395	169
Tonopah	Station House	On US-95	175
Verdi	Boomtown	I-80 exit 4	172
Verdi	Gold Ranch	I-80 exit 4	172

| W. Wendover | Montego Bay | I-80/UT border | 178 |
| Winnemucca | Model T | I-80 exit 178 | 182 |

New Mexico

City	Casino Name	Nearest Highway	Page
Casa Blanca	Dancing Eagle	I-40 exit 108	187
San Felipe	San Felipe	I-25 exit 252	189

New York

City	Casino Name	Nearest Highway	Page
Verona	Turning Stone	I-90 exit 33	196

North Dakota

City	Casino Name	Nearest Highway	Page
Belcourt	Sky Dancer*	I-29 exit 203	204
Fort Yates	Prairie Knights	I-94 at Mandan	202
Hankinson	Dakota Magic	I-29, exit 1	202
New Town	Four Bears	I-94 exit 61	205
Spirit Lake	Spirit Lake	I-29 exit 141	203

Oklahoma

City	Casino Name	Nearest Highway	Page
Concho	Lucky Star*	I-40 exit 125	214
Claremore	Cherokee/W. Rogers	I-44 exit 255	211
Devol	Comanche Red River*	I-44 exit 4	222
Lawton	Comanche Nation*	I-44 exit 37	221
Miami	Quapaw	I-44 exit 313	208
Newkirk	Kaw Nation*	I-35 exit 222	213
Red Rock	7 Clans*	I-35 exit 194	213
Shawnee	Fire Lake	I-40 exit 186	216

Oregon

City	Casino Name	Nearest Highway	Page
Canyonville	Seven Feathers	I-5 exit 99	224
Pendleton	Wildhorse	I-84 exit 216	226

South Dakota

City	Casino Name	Nearest Highway	Page
Flandreau	Royal River	I-29 exit 114	233
Mobridge	Grand River	On US-12	235
Pickstown	Fort Randall*	I-90 exit 310	234
Watertown	Dakota Sioux *	I-29 exit 185	232

Washington

City	Casino Name	Nearest Highway	Page
Anacortes	Northern Lights	I-5 exit 230	241
Chewelah	Chewelah	US-395	246
Davenport	Two Rivers	I-90 exit 277	245
Deming	Nooksack*	I-5 exit 255	242
Rochester	Lucky Eagle *	I-5 exit 88	237

Wisconsin

City	Casino Name	Nearest Highway	Page
Black River Falls	Majestic Pines *	I-94 exit 116	252
Bowler	Mohican North	US-41/Hwy-29	254
Danbury	Hole in the Wall	Hwy-35/Hwy-77	256
Green Bay	Oneida *	Hwy-41/Rt-172	253
Keshena	Menominee	US-41/Hwy-29	253
Lac du Flameau	Lake of Torches	I-39/US-51 No.	257
Nekoosa	Rainbow*	I-39 exit 136	252
Odanah	Bad River *	On US-2	258
Turtle Lake	St. Croix	On US-8	255

Index

T

U

V

W

X Y Z